Advance Praise for

LEADERSHIP IN THE EYE OF THE STORM

"No organization – large or small, private or public sector, or not-for-profit – will survive the good times or the bad without strong leadership from top to bottom. Employees must have trust in their leaders, and that doesn't suddenly appear through osmosis when a tragedy occurs. It is earned through months and years of daily interaction – in formal and informal settings. *Leadership in the Eye of the Storm* drives those and many other critical points home for the reader."

Chris D. Lewis, Commissioner,
Ontario Provincial Police, Retired

"*Leadership in the Eye of the Storm* provides a very effective methodology that can be used in any crisis management situation. More importantly, the leadership lessons provide managers and leaders with valuable techniques to enhance their personal style. A definite must-read for all high potential employees in any organization."

Jim Lovie, Executive Vice President,
Rogers Communication Inc., Retired

"Bill Tibbo's new book underlines the core of great leadership – that of being human with employees especially during a crisis. His examples of characteristics of exceptional leaders with whom he has worked are vivid and helpful to the reader. His wealth of experience in the field of crisis management is vast and diverse in both public and private sector global organizations. This book is a must-read for all organizational leaders to fully understand the depth of crises on the emotional and physical health of their employees."

Dr Tom Reynolds, Executive and Team Coach,
Former International Director of EAP for BMO group of companies and
Warren Shepell (now Morneau Shepell) EAP Consulting Company

"This sensitive and very practical guide to sustaining crises emphasizes over and over the need to deal with the emotional needs of the people affected and how good leaders instinctively know and identify with their employees. Facing crises in politics and in the corporate world for over 40 years, I would have greatly benefited from this well-documented work."

Patrick Gossage, former Press Secretary to Pierre
Trudeau and Founder and Chair, Media Profile

"Bill Tibbo's *Leadership in the Eye of the Storm* urges business leaders to understand crises as human events and encourages those leaders to focus on their people – before, during, and after a crisis. In his direct and engaging style, Bill brings this guidance to life through a fine balance of theory, anecdotes, and real-life examples, with special emphasis on the emotional needs of employees."

Neil Wilson, President and CEO, NAV Canada

"Bill Tibbo has successfully guided a broad range of business leaders and organizations through some of the largest crises in recent memory. He shows that there can be no effective response to crisis management at any stage that does not focus on and include the people involved. *Leadership in the Eye of the Storm* is a practical guide to crisis management, with a focus on human capital."

Sean Forgie, Senior Vice President, SRD Claimspro – Special Risks Division

"Any CEO facing a crisis should make Bill Tibbo their first call. Bill's decades of hands-on experience leading organizations through some of the greatest catastrophes imaginable have given him hard-earned wisdom balanced with unerring compassion for people. Mixed with keen insights and captivating real-life examples, *Leadership in the Eye of the Storm* brilliantly captures Bill's philosophy of putting people first during times of crisis. This is a book that should find a place on every leader's must-read list."

"I truly enjoyed Bill's open, honest, and insightful view into the qualities that are important in allowing leaders to lead. He has been very effective in connecting the dots from emotional to practical to actionable in a way that many business books attempt but do not always achieve. It is most refreshing to see his vocational discipline applied to business leadership, not only in mega disasters, but also in daily applications. Clearly his extensive experience has created a book for all of us to use in day-to-day life and business situations."

"Disasters and traumatic events can occur at any moment and have the potential to significantly disrupt or even destroy your business. Under-standing and leveraging the human element as vividly described by Bill Tibbo will give your business a competitive advantage when facing these events and will give your employees a sense of calm and confi-dence to quickly and effectively restore your operations."

"Bill outlines in simple, easy-to-read, and down-to-earth examples how to lead and be led in a crisis – a must for any organization that is focused on the long-term health of the company and its success. *Leadership in the Eye of the Storm* clearly illustrates that the most important capital any corporation can possess in a crisis is the human kind."

"A leader is the heartbeat of an organization, and in a crisis a lead-er's actions can either fuel the flames or provide a calm and steady path to recovery. This book is a step-by-step guide for leaders who want to provide compassionate, thoughtful, and ultimately success-ful management through a crisis by first addressing the most impor-tant aspect of a company – its people."

LEADERSHIP IN THE EYE OF THE STORM

LEADERSHIP IN THE EYE OF THE STORM

Putting Your People First in a Crisis

BILL TIBBO

UNIVERSITY OF TORONTO PRESS
Toronto Buffalo London

© University of Toronto Press 2016
Rotman-UTP Publishing
University of Toronto Press
Toronto Buffalo London
www.utppublishing.com
Printed in Canada

ISBN 978-1-4426-4994-1

∞ Printed on acid-free, 100% post-consumer recycled paper with
vegetable-based inks.

Library and Archives Canada Cataloguing in Publication

Tibbo, Bill, 1960–, author
Leadership in the eye of the storm : putting your people first in a crisis /
Bill Tibbo.

Includes bibliographical references and index.
ISBN 978-1-4426-4994-1 (hardcover)

1. Crisis management. 2. Leadership. I. Title.

HD49.T52   2016   658.4′056   C2016-903548-4

University of Toronto Press acknowledges the financial assistance to its
publishing program of the Canada Council for the Arts and the Ontario
Arts Council, an agency of the Government of Ontario.

 Canada Council
for the Arts   Conseil des Arts
du Canada

 ONTARIO ARTS COUNCIL
CONSEIL DES ARTS DE L'ONTARIO
an Ontario government agency
un organisme du gouvernement de l'Ontario

Funded by the   Financé par le
Government   gouvernement
of Canada   du Canada   Canadä

To the three men who have taught me life's important lessons:
My father, Hugh Tibbo, who taught me about bravery
My father-in-law, Bill Gillespie, who taught me about loyalty
My brother George Tibbo, who taught me about integrity

Contents

PART THREE: LEADERSHIP LESSONS

Acknowledgments

Over the three-and-a-half decades of my career, I have worked with thousands of people who have influenced my understanding of trauma, crisis response, and human emotion. I am grateful to all the men and women who have freed up their time, opened their offices and boardrooms to me, and shared their heartfelt, personal accounts of what they and the people around them have been through. In every case, I know that it was difficult and painful to recall these experiences, and I hope that everyone I have worked with knows how much I respect and value their input. Sharing in those recollections has been one of the most rewarding and informative experiences of my life.

More than twenty organizational leaders were interviewed for this project, and four case studies were chosen to be represented in the final version of the book. This selection process was not easy given the restrictions of space and our desire to represent different industries, including American and Canadian companies and both public and private organizations. While only a few cases were included in their entirety, I want to thank the other leaders who took the time to share their experiences with me – your insights have informed my work and the ideas that appear in this book.

Over my career, I have been called into 150–200 organizations per year all over the world. Those experiences have educated me about the most important considerations for effective crisis response because I have had the opportunity to work with exceptional leaders. I would like to thank a few of them in particular for allowing me to support their teams and learn from their leadership: Neil Wilson, Audrey Costello, Rick Foley, Commissioner Vince Hawks, Renee Jarvis, Kevin Maher, Don Poynter, Mara Volpini, Cindy Capstick, Joanne Martin, Andrea Challis, Rose Sones, Chief Sandra Moore, Sharon Marshall, Jim Lovie, Anita Boyle Evans, Darren Slind, Rhonda Barnat, Annette Jones, Ellen Stafford-Sigg, Susan Gretchko, and Chisanga Puta-Chekwe.

To the four leaders whose case studies are used in this book – Tom Spedding, Bonnie Adamson, Nancy Tower, and Lyne Wilson – thank you! I hope that my account has represented your organization well and the esteem that I have for the four of you. I am very proud to convey the lessons of your experiences to a larger audience and grateful for your participation in this project.

I also want to thank several people who have taught me leadership lessons in the context of our professional relationships and personal friendship: Ross MacPhail, Alton Dingee, Darren Brown, Phil Allan, Doug Hayes, Norval Wener, Dr Steve Stokl, Glenn Marais, Patrick Gossage, Dr Vidoll Regisford, and Eric Schwendau. Each of you has strategically positioned a significant brick in my wall.

Over ten years ago, my family lost a central member: my brother-in-law Dan McIntyre. Dan was a pioneer in the field of human rights in Canada. Though he was only with us for fifty years, he taught many of us the true meaning of decency and respect. Your words show up in my behaviour regularly, Dan. Thank you.

I am indebted to the team who helped bring this book to life. My editors, Karen Sumner and Warren Lang, were patient, cautious where necessary, and enthusiastic at all times, and I relied on their wisdom, insight, hard work, and determination throughout the process. Jennifer DiDomenico and the team at Rotman-UTP Publishing saw the merit in this project from the beginning, and their professionalism and care helped make the final product what it is today. Ron Dimock and Sangeetha Punniyamoorthy offered legal advice and insight that was sage and constructive, often easing my burden and providing much needed direction.

Finally, I am forever thankful to have a partner in life who has been with me from graduate school. We have been through a series of metamorphoses together, facing highs and lows, great dreams achieved, and some visions failed. She never once questioned when my phone went off in the middle of an idle night or family gathering and I had to leave to go to someone's aid. Janet, you have been there for me and our beautiful children from the beginning. I know I married up. Thank you for saying "yes." And to our children, Gillian and Matthew: my goal in life has always been to do the right thing and chart a course worth following. You have been my reason for doing so.

Part One

People-Focused Crisis Leadership

Chapter One

Introduction

One secret act of self-denial, one sacrifice of inclination to duty, is worth all of the mere good thoughts, warm feelings, and passionate prayers in which idle men indulge themselves.

John Henry Newman

Certain images remain fixed in our memories forever. The sights, sounds, and smells are as vivid today as they were at the time of the event. For me, one such image is standing in a corporate boardroom in Midtown Manhattan on 14 September 2001, looking out over the city as smoke rose from what would later be dubbed Ground Zero. It was as if the sky itself had become a smoldering monument to the people who died three days earlier during the attacks on the World Trade Center.

I was in New York leading a large team of Canadian mental health professionals to assist several companies in getting their businesses back on track. There was so much about the event that I did not understand, including why anyone would do that sort of thing. I also had all the questions that come with my work, such as "What do people need to carry on?" and "How do all these businesses get back on track?"

My job was to support thousands of employees and their families affected by the disaster as they tried to put their lives back together. As I stood looking out the window, I remember thinking that they all had something in common with people all across New York, the country, and the world who were collectively reeling from the shock, grief, loss, and after-effects of the attacks.

They needed to heal.

A Crisis Is a Human Event

In the business continuity management field, there are various terms used to refer to an incident, such as "disaster," "emergency," "tragedy," and "event." To me, all those categories can be included under the word "crisis." A crisis is essentially *a complex and unexpected event that creates instability, damage, threat, or risk to the company and its people.* In my experience, the most important thing to understand about a crisis is that people are involved. Like the tree that falls in the forest and makes no sound if no one is there to hear it, damage is only relevant if it has an impact on people. If an abandoned building crumbles to the ground, a vacant house burns down, or a drone crashes in the desert, the damage is limited. But when people are involved, events take on a negative, even tragic, quality for leaders, employees, and other stakeholders, including customers and clients, suppliers, government authorities, and the media. A tragedy is measured in human terms.

Crisis response is a complex process in any organization. It involves everything from restoring and protecting data to rebuilding factories to re-establishing the supply chain. But in my experience, as you will see throughout this book, the primary feature of a successful crisis response process is helping people cope. A crisis has massive personal, mental, emotional, and intellectual repercussions for the people involved, even for those who were only marginally connected to the event itself. Organizations that take the time to carefully and fully support each employee's personal recovery are the most successful at getting their operations back on track and ensuring the long-term success of their business.

If employees feel supported, they are able to invest in recovering quickly and effectively. On the contrary, if staff members are treated as objects and not involved in the process of recovery, businesses suffer, both in the short and the long term. The integrated nature of emotional and operational recovery flows from a basic reality: every aspect of an organization involves people. Even the most profit-driven, bottom-line focused managers in the world are smart to beat a path to profitability through the realm of employee needs. Business continuity and crisis response processes need to include a significant focus on taking care of people, because the sooner everyone is functioning – connected to the goals of the company and pulling together in the name of the cause – the sooner the company can get back to doing what it does best.

Implemented properly, a people-focused approach to crisis management will not only ensure that the recovery process goes well, but can also lead to greater solidity and community than what existed prior to the crisis, including increased loyalty, decreased absenteeism, improved morale, and a strong, cohesive team.

The most successful organizations excel at focusing on the emotional realities of their employees. When leaders see the situation through the eyes of their employees – and try to meet core emotional, psychological, and social needs – they ensure the long-term success of their businesses in ways that a narrow emphasis on profit and profitability can never achieve. Employees who have a strong sense of their place in the organization and tangible evidence that they are connected to the company community will work hard to promote company success.

Recognizing the people in your business as capital – human capital – can help clarify and galvanize your thinking. This is not to say that you should conceive of your people as objects. It simply means that no matter how labour intensive your "product" is, regarding the people in your organization as your greatest asset sets you well on your way towards re-establishing the effective operation of your business. By way of analogy, think of a professional athletic team. No success can be achieved without the right players, and the management pays and treats the players as their greatest asset, supporting them and providing all the feedback they need to develop and thrive. We should think of our employees in the same way. They are the cornerstone of success in any organization, and taking care of them is the key to getting your business back on track. Employees have to feel that they belong and, most of all, that they are connected to you and the organization.

Crisis response processes often conjure references to Maslow's famous hierarchy of needs because quite often there is pressure to begin by dealing with the basics of life, such as food, safety, and shelter. Employees frequently need assistance with the essential requirements of living: finding a place to sleep, knowing where their loved ones are, and sorting out whether they will have a job to come back to. These needs are very real, and not much of any organizational recovery can occur until they have been addressed.

But soon after the initial damage and physical risks are under control, employees begin dealing with the far more complex social and emotional needs that reside further up Maslow's pyramid. Supporting employees who are coping with shock, confusion, and grief is a complex and ongoing process. Everything that happens in a crisis rejuvenation effort has to take those needs into account.

Our Need to Be Led

One of the most difficult aspects of a crisis is that things will never be the same again. Any significant event involves "second order" change, where something has been irreversibly altered for the organization and the way its staff experience daily life. A great challenge in dealing with tragedy, loss, and confusion is trying to find a new way of living and working. People struggle to accept that, no matter what, some things cannot go back to the way they were before. Life is no longer business as usual. This is why employees focus on the people in charge: they are looking for a North Star to lead them out of chaos towards a new future.

In my work with organizations, I ask leaders to accept two basic principles about their approach to crisis planning, response, and recovery. First, leadership is the defining feature of an effective recovery; and second, the leadership team needs to continually assess every element of the recovery process from a human perspective. These two principles are the basis of what I call people-focused crisis leadership, which is grounded in a business rejuvenation core principle: **if you rebuild your people, you rebuild your organization**.

During a crisis and throughout the immediate response period, a focus on people's needs can take many forms. The focus may be on providing group debriefing sessions to help everyone cope with their losses. It might be on keeping everyone informed about the progress of the recovery plan. Sometimes the focus is on reintegrating employees back into their work at just the right pace so they can adjust successfully. Or it could be on finding individual employees a pet care service to tend to their dog or a place for their aging mother to stay so they can come to work with one less concern on their mind.

At times, the organizations I work with struggle to accept that focusing on the needs of employees is essential to getting their operations back up and running. They focus immediately on getting the factory working or assessing the costs of replacing damaged capital, even though those issues will take care of themselves when the leadership helps the employees heal and cope. In thirty years of advising organizations about how to repair and rebuild after a devastating event, I have worked on four continents and been exposed to hundreds of crises. Experience has shown me that effective, people-focused leadership is the critical element that separates successful renewal and recovery from ongoing confusion and loss. When this kind of leadership is absent, it is very difficult for people to carry on.

As an example, I was once called to a retail banking location in Toronto after an armed robbery. One significant cause of the staff's trauma came not from the actual crime, which was terrifying in itself, but from the manager's response: he hid under a desk throughout the robbery while everyone else suffered at the hands of the assailants. The sense of abandonment cut deeply. In another instance,

I worked with the displaced staff of a financial institution in the Caribbean after a tropical storm had devastated their community. Their director had fled the country while they remained on location, sleeping on the floor of the office because their homes had been destroyed. Deserted by a leader concerned only with his personal comfort and safety, the staff were expected to begin the business rejuvenation process without him. The despair in their voices and their need for direction were the most immediate and visceral indications of their stress. A third example comes from a small moment during an epidemic in Toronto. As I walked through the halls of a large hospital that I was advising, I fell in step with a support services employee who was going my way. We began to talk about the staff and the impact that this event was having on the hospital community. Through my N95 surgical mask, I asked, "What does the CEO look like? I haven't had a chance to meet him yet." My masked companion, who had worked in the hospital for six years, replied, "I don't know – I have never seen him either."

About This Book

Leadership in the Eye of the Storm was born from my desire to record and share the qualities of amazing leaders I have worked with over the years. My career has allowed me to work closely with hundreds of leaders in as many different situations as you can imagine. As a result, I have developed a catalogue of examples, ideas, and approaches that successful leaders use. I have found that those who put their people first in a crisis are highly successful in their efforts to rebuild their organization.

My intention in writing this book is to provide insight into one of the most important parts of business rejuvenation efforts: how leaders should approach the human resources issues that arise within their organization. Drawing on my background in trauma response and crisis-based employee assistance programs (EAPs), I want to offer a unique perspective on crisis response that illustrates the central role that employees' emotional, psychological, and social needs play. I also want to explore how organizations that make those needs a priority can excel. The book is intended to complement existing business continuity management literature and theory, and to help leaders develop an approach to crisis response that is effective and sustainable.

This book is intended for business and organizational leaders who are, in some way, responsible for the welfare of employees during a crisis. Readers could include a C-level executive who oversees the entire response process, of which human resources issues are one part, as well as a team member who has been charged with the exclusive responsibility of looking out for the employees. My reader might be a human resources leader, a government official, an EAP professional, a police services employee, an international development worker, an executive, or a manager in almost any kind of corporate setting. My emphasis is on applicable ideas and useful techniques that I have learned and observed throughout my career. I want this book to be a compelling read and a lasting resource that will help you to excel when a storm arrives.

The evidence provided in this book, which is also the basis for all my speaking and training work, is drawn primarily from three decades of crisis response counselling and from the experiences of the four leaders I have profiled. It is not loaded with theoretical or statistical models. I have taken this approach because I have learned that the human side of crisis response is highly personal and subjective. The nuances involved in caring for people's needs can only really be explained and understood by examining the experiences and approaches of those who have led the way. Evidence drawn from reflection and personal perspective is relevant and useful for leaders who want to understand the human side of crisis response.

Throughout this book, I have emphasized stories wherever possible, and have included ideas about crisis leadership collected from direct observation or from conversation with leaders whom I know. During the preparation for this book, I interviewed four leaders who fit two key criteria: 1) their approach to crisis response illustrated some aspect of my people-focused crisis leadership theory, and 2) their stories could be told here in full. My intention was to provide rich insights from a few leaders whom I could represent in depth. All these leaders give a personal account of their situation rather than an independently verified testimonial, and I have, in some places, paraphrased to ensure a level of readability that is sometimes difficult to achieve with direct transcriptions. All four leaders have read and approved this version of their story.

Part one outlines the core ideas of people-focused crisis leadership. Chapter one is an introduction to my theory. Chapter two is a discussion of the critical role that leadership plays in helping employees recover from an event. Chapters three and four emphasize two particular needs that regularly stand out and require attention: employees' emotional lives and effective communication. Part two introduces the four leaders whom I profile and explores key approaches to each of four stages in a crisis response: before, during, after, and reflection. Part three expands on the lessons of the book by looking at how my ideas apply to everyday leadership situations and reflecting on my experiences in the aftermath of the 9/11 attacks. Throughout, I have arranged the chapters as much as possible so that they begin with key concepts to consider, outline how those ideas appear in a crisis, and then offer specific techniques relevant to crisis response.

This book is about putting the needs of your people at the centre of the business rejuvenation process. In my experience, leaders who look people in the eye and hold their employees in mind at all times are the ones most able to rise from the ashes of crisis and embark on the path towards a prosperous future. I have worked with many, many leaders in situations that shook their workplaces and personal lives to the core. The good ones lifted their chins to the challenge, reached out a hand to their team, and said, "It's okay – we are in this together." In every one of those cases, the leaders – sometimes by instinct, sometimes by trial and error, and always through guts and determination – were listening closely when their employees said, "This is what we need."

LEADERSHIP SUMMARY

Key Concept
• People-focused crisis leadership emphasizes the importance of putting your people first in a crisis. If you rebuild your people, you rebuild your organization.

Definition of a Crisis
• A crisis is a complex and unexpected event that creates instability, damage, threat, or risk to the company and its people.

Key Features of a Crisis
• Crisis is a human event in which damage is measured in human terms.
• Leadership focuses on helping employees cope with social and emotional needs.
• Second order change means that things cannot return to how they were before.

Chapter Two

Someone to Watch Over Me: The Centrality of Leadership

The real sovereign of the state are the people of the state. If a ruler is not a servant of the people then he is not the ruler.

Mohandas K. Gandhi

Do you remember what you were doing at around 9 a.m. on 11 September 2001? I suspect that is not a difficult question to answer. But do you remember what was going through your head? Or what you did for the rest of the day? No doubt, like the majority of the population, you were shocked, paid close attention to the news, and pulled your loved ones close to make sure they were safe. All perfectly normal reactions that I had as well.

Until my phone rang.

The call came from Family Guidance International (FGI), an EAP provider that regularly reached out to me when a company was in crisis and needed support for its employees. Responding to the massive need for employee assistance and aware that there would not be enough trauma counsellors in the immediate area to help, FGI asked me to put together a team of fifty mental health professionals to travel immediately to New York to assist a dozen Manhattan-based companies. By the next morning, my team and I were headed south towards Ground Zero, travelling by bus because all air traffic had been shut down.

Sorting out the logistics and approach as we went along, we made our way to New Jersey, our initial headquarters, and drove onto the island every morning to spend nineteen to twenty hours a day supporting, guiding, counselling, and debriefing groups of workers. Over the course of the three weeks following the attacks, we supported close to 2,300 people.

For many members of my team, this assignment was the largest scale crisis they had ever dealt with, especially given the violent nature of the attacks and the widespread shock they caused. An act of war in a civic context was staggering to almost everyone. Most of us, including seasoned crisis response experts, were completely overwhelmed by the emotional impact of the events. As team leader, I had to track the strain of the work on the counsellors. In some cases, I had to relieve people of their duties and send them home after ten days or so because the work was far too demanding. There was just too much to process.

But our difficulty processing what was happening paled in comparison to the suffering of the people we were there to support. The traumatized employees we worked with during those three weeks had every imaginable emotional reaction to the crisis: they were shocked, overwhelmed, confused, angry, stunned, and numb. It was the most devastating experience they had ever faced.

In the sessions, we often simply gave employees a forum in which to begin working through their reactions. Many times, they began by trying to reconstruct the events so that they could make sense of the facts. They asked questions like, "Did that happen before or after the second plane hit?" and "When I was trying to get down the back stairs, where were you?" and "Where did you go after we got down to street level?"

Once they had some sense of the details of the event itself, they tried to sort out how they felt and make sense of what they were going through: "I go home at night and wonder if I am crazy. The room seems to spin, and I don't know what to feel, and my mood changes all the time." In many cases, people simply needed reassurance that what they were experiencing was normal and that others were having similar reactions.

Throughout our time in New York, we listened at length to employees who were raw, confused, and searching for answers. While it was all happening, my colleagues and I had very little opportunity to pull back the lens and develop perspective. Most of the people who were on my team will tell you that this experience was a defining one in their careers and their lives. But only after our time there was over were we able to make some sense of what had happened.

Sitting together on the bus back to Ontario, or in the many, many conversations that followed once we were home, we connected what we had seen in New York to our experiences helping other organizations navigate through crises. We saw that while 9/11 was larger and more intense, the fundamental nature of the response was the same. As employees grappled with the enormity of their loss and tried to cope with the threat to their safety and security, they returned over and over again to expressions of need directed towards their leaders. In a crisis people seek reassurance, direction, and information from the figures they believe can provide those things, and the significance of leadership becomes magnified.

Leadership Is Essential

In a crisis, leadership is the single most important force for change and recovery. The qualities of the leader and the approach taken shape everything. In their article "Crisis Leadership and Why It Matters," Erika Hayes James and Lynn Perry Wooten (authors of *Leading under Pressure: From Surviving to Thriving Before, During and After a Crisis*) explain:

> Crisis leadership matters because leaders of organizations and nations *can* make a difference in the extent to which people are affected by a crisis. Crisis leadership matters, because, in its absence, the stakeholders who are adversely affected by the crisis cannot truly recover from the damaging event. Crisis leadership matters, because despite the damage that is caused by a crisis, effective leadership is the one factor

that creates the potential for a company and its stakeholders to be better off following the crisis than it was before the crisis.[1]

I think leadership is at the core of crisis response, because connection is at the core of the human experience. At all levels of experience, in every socio-economic and cultural context, and in all stages of life, people have a need to connect. We are social animals oriented towards attachment with other people. From the moment of birth, we build bonds with our caregivers. It is a matter of physical and emotional survival. As adults, we seek attachments in friendships, in romantic relationships, at work, on sports teams, in book clubs, and so on. This need is primary and primal, and in a crisis it takes on a particular flavour because of the uncertainty and insecurity we face. We turn towards the leaders with the hope and expectation that they will offset the disorienting effects of the event.

In psychology, this effect – reaching out to a secure figure in our lives for stability and reassurance – is referred to as attachment theory. In his blog *Transforming Leadership*, leadership development innovator Gene Early summarizes the theory's relevance for crisis response:

> Attachment theory posits that distress, crisis, and isolation (to name a few conditions) activate at least three areas of attachment need within individuals. The *first* is the need to draw close to an attachment figure whose presence comforts and/or soothes the anxiety of the individual. The *second* is the need for a safe haven in relationship with an attachment figure, i.e. a place of safety, protection, and support in the midst of this experience. The *third* is a secure base from which to engage in exploratory, creative, and productive activity.[2]

Even well-adjusted adults faced with the uncertainty, confusion, and loss created in a crisis are reassured by the presence of a strong leader who helps them believe things will be okay.

Our need to attach to the boss comes in part from the significant role that work plays in forming our identity. As American philosopher and psychologist John Dewey observed, "To find out what one is fitted to do, and to secure an opportunity to do it, is the key to happiness." This is why one of our first questions when we meet someone new is often, "What do you do for a living?" The emotional importance of their work has been evident with the thousands of employees I have supported over the years. It shapes their sense of who they are and informs how they feel on any given day. Many employees adopt the values of the company as their own, shaping their personal world view around the workplace emphasis. They tend to find their "tribe" in the workplace: people of similar energy and interests. When our work is the right fit for us and we excel at it, we feel good about our lives. When our work is a burden to us and we are at odds with our colleagues, we suffer.

This reality was on display when I became involved in an investigation into a series of infant injuries at the Hospital for Sick Children in Toronto. I happened upon a nurse who was holding a premature baby in her arms. She was lifting the baby to her face and trying to get the child to smile. I stood and watched the paradoxical mix of grim determination and soft affection on the nurse's face as she focused on getting a reaction from the infant. In time, after a concerted effort, the child smiled. Though mired in an environment of concern and stress, the nurse beamed back, her joy evident. Such is the emotional power of success in our work.

The boss also matters because when competent, committed, and inspiring people point the way, we feel a surge of energy. Nothing is quite like being called to serve: life has a sense of purpose and focus. Ask people why they love their work, and see how quickly they refer to the leadership as a reason for their satisfaction. Our attentiveness to leadership is evident in everyday exchanges. Imagine a handful of typical scenarios: someone comes home from work and answers the "How was your day?" question with a two-hour narrative about what the boss did or did not do; a parent is upset and agitated about a decision made by the convener of a local soccer league or school council; or we read about the government and reach conclusions about what they are, or are not, doing to lead us. We are all interested in connecting to leaders as people. Having a direct relationship with the boss – even when fairly simple and superficial – is highly important to people. The leader is the personification of the cause – a living and breathing embodiment of workplace values and purpose. We all tend to think in people terms, and our ability to cope with the uncertainty, confusion, and fear associated with a crisis is partly a consequence of our connection to the boss. Just think of the role that former New York Mayor Rudy Giuliani played following the 9/11 attacks. He was the personification of the efforts of a city rising, literally and figuratively, from the ashes. People everywhere connected to him, and the cause came to life in his commitment to be highly visible and present.

Leaders are also critical because they create a sense of purpose and direction by establishing priorities and solidifying goals. As Field Marshal Bernard Law Montgomery said, leadership is the "capacity and will to rally men and women to a common purpose and the character which inspires confidence." Our deep need for meaning, purpose, and direction is fulfilled by effective leaders and is evident in situations where people rally around a leader in the name of a cause.

The need for meaning and purpose is equally evident in situations where people are led astray. Just think about the young men who flew those planes into the World Trade Center. Following the direction of a leader to the point where you turn yourself into a deadly weapon is the human need for meaning and purpose gone horribly wrong. Since 9/11, research about what makes people join terrorist organizations has increased around the world. In November 2009, *Monitor on Psychology* published an article by Tori DeAngelis titled "Understanding Terrorism" that identified the desire for "meaning and personal significance" as a primary driver in the decision to "enlist." The article also pointed to "the need to take action" and a "heightened sense of identity" as key considerations for the often abjectly poor young men who join terrorist cells.[3] Those phrases also describe young people in North America who join gangs. Both the Los Angeles Police Department and Gangfree, an anti-gang social organization in California, offer identity, status, purpose, and a sense of family as primary draws for youth who commit to the gang culture. Our deep need for leadership draws many into a life of menace and violence.

Accepting responsibility to provide meaning, purpose, and direction is important for all leaders. When I work with executive teams, I suggest that they think about the relationship between themselves, their employees, and their shared goals in terms of a simple equation: one who is willing to be led + one who is willing to lead = one newfound direction. When leaders emphasize employee engagement and provide strong direction, the equation can come to life – especially if they involve others in finding solutions to problems. In particular, I emphasize that the right-hand side of the equation – newfound direction – has to be well established and aggressively defended. Everyone needs distinct outcomes to work towards. Once these goals are identified, energy and creativity can be harnessed, and workers can be empowered to find creative solutions. Think about the scene in Ron Howard's film *Apollo 13* when the carbon dioxide levels on the lunar capsule carrying Jim Lovell and his crew are rising and a group of engineers have to figure out how to create a contraption that will fit a square filter into a round aperture. The team arrives in a work room and dumps several cardboard boxes full of materials on the table. Their leader then explains that these materials are the only ones they have to work with because that is all that the astronauts have access to. The end goal is fixed: create a filter that will save the crew. But the solution is entirely up to the group responding to the clear direction of the leadership. The situation is summarized in the lead engineer's opening remarks to his team: "The people upstairs have handed us this one, and we've got to come through."[4]

Serve Your People

My approach to crisis response is to focus on the needs of the people in the organization. As a result, it was a natural and obvious fit for me to follow the tenets of "servant leadership" – the well-known philosophy advocated by figures such as Gandhi and Martin Luther King Jr in which the leader is a servant first. In his biography of King, Marshall Frady explains that the need for a strong leader among the members of the Montgomery Improvement Association (MIA) preceded King's aspiration to offer himself as a key figure in the civil rights movement:

> The question then arose as to who was to be put forward as the leader of this whole affair. With surprising swiftness, though at twenty-six he still struck some as "more like a boy than a man" ... King found himself the only person nominated. Stunned, when asked if he would accept the position King responded with minimal assent, "If you think I can render some service, I will."[5]

Many kinds of leadership are useful and acceptable during the normal course of business, but when a crisis occurs, leadership that follows the needs of the people tends to be the most effective. As Center for Servant Leadership member Margaret Wheatley describes:

> There are many patterns out there about leadership, about people, about motivation, about human development ... [T]he essential pattern is that when we are together, more becomes possible. When we are together, joy is available. In the midst of a world that is insane, that will continue to surprise us with new outrages ... in the midst of that future, the gift is each other.[6]

In his 2010 essay titled "Character and Servant Leadership," Larry C. Spears summarizes Robert Greenleaf's tenets of servant leadership, all of which are essential for crisis response. Greenleaf is considered the founder of the modern servant leadership movement, and Spears's summary of his servant-first qualities includes *listening* – taking the time to really understand what followers are saying and care about; *empathy* – connecting to the workers as people and validating their humanness even if their performance in a given part of their work is not ideal; *healing* – moving to a healthier and more whole state of being for the self and the organization; *commitment to the growth of people* – placing an emphasis on increasing everyone's capacity; and *building community* – creating the conditions that will promote cultural and social connections in the organization.[7]

Robert Greenleaf's ground-breaking work on servant leadership extended beyond the individual to the institution. In a subsection of "What Is Servant Leadership?" titled "The Institution as Servant," he challenged leaders to conceive of the role of organizations in a society in a new way:

> This is my thesis: caring for persons, the more able and the less able serving each other, is the rock upon which a good society is built. Whereas, until recently, caring was largely person to person, now most of it is mediated through institutions – often large, complex, powerful, impersonal; not always competent; sometimes corrupt. If a better society is to be built, one that is more just and more loving, one that provides greater creative opportunity for its people, then the most open course is to raise both the capacity to serve and the very performance as servant of existing major institutions by new regenerative forces operating within them.[8]

Greenleaf's emphasis and the core ideas of servant leadership have proven themselves to be essential in all the crises I have seen. An autocratic or command-and-control approach to leadership simply does not work when a genuine crisis hits. You have to approach leadership in a way that brings people together and promotes closeness, care, and belonging. You can't be thinking, "These are the people who work for me." You have to think, "These are the people I work for."

In his 1999 book *It's How You Play the Game: The 12 Leadership Principles of Dean Smith*, David Chadwick profiles the esteemed college basketball coach and his philosophy of leadership. Chadwick calls Dean Smith's first rule of leadership "the reciprocal law of loyalty."

He says, "If you are loyal to your people, your people will be loyal to you."[9] A leader's loyalty to his or her people can often be hard for workers to see and experience on an ongoing basis, but it is one of the foundational qualities that needs to be in place before a storm comes. Creating a culture of trust is essential. I remember watching Dr Jim MacLean, CEO of Markham Stouffville Hospital, put his mask, gown, and gloves on night after night, because he visited the most infected areas of his hospital throughout the sudden acute respiratory syndrome (SARS) epidemic to see how his people were doing. He was a loved man before the epidemic, but became that much more esteemed after the masks came off. As servant leadership supporter Stephen Covey says, "To value oneself and, at the same time, subordinate oneself to the higher purposes and principles is the paradoxical essence of highest humanity and the foundation of effective leadership."[10]

When an organization puts the needs of its employees first, the effect is astonishing – as it was in 1999 when I was in Istanbul, Turkey, helping Procter & Gamble (P&G) deal with the fallout of the earthquake that caused widespread devastation and dislocation, including the deaths of close to 40,000 people.

Earthquakes are terrible things. They take decades to recover from, and they can damage people and businesses in fundamental and overwhelming ways. P&G is a unique organization with an explicit commitment to acknowledging and valuing the integrated relationship between the organization and its employees. When faced with hundreds of decisions about how to allocate time, personnel, and money to manage the relief efforts and subsequent recovery, P&G put the needs of its employees first. From dealing with factories that had come to a halt or were severely damaged to supporting workers who had lost their homes and were having trouble finding food, the P&G leadership team was under constant pressure to prioritize and innovate. They were impressive in dealing with the crisis, because their focus the entire time was on remembering that people are not machines.

Initially, P&G managers took care of basic needs by providing food and shelter. Then they set up a building supply fund to help employees begin to get their homes back up and running. They offered extensive EAP and medical support. Throughout the process, they resisted the urge to get their plants up and running too quickly. Chief among their approaches was a commitment to progressive re-entry as the company's production began to come back online, which involved letting employees set the pace of their own return to work. The leadership knew that success would come with continued effort over time and that the focus needed to be on helping people get back to being fully functional rather than pushing them to work when they might not be ready. This approach developed immeasurable loyalty among the workforce and a highly productive atmosphere once individuals were back at work. Workers were left feeling good about the company, even when their personal circumstances made work a marginal part of their lives. They were then able to take that sense of connection and confidence home to their families, which widened the circle of coping and grew into a sense of hope. Belief in the future and initial success began with the leadership team's approach and flowed all the way into the homes of the P&G employees. This would not have been possible if the company had been pushing to get more widgets out of the machine.

LEADERSHIP SUMMARY

Key Concepts
- Employees need to feel attached to the leader to feel confident that recovery is possible.
- People connect to people before the cause.
- Leaders need to focus on serving their people.
- A confident workforce connected to its leader is motivated and capable of ensuring success after a setback.
- Leaders provide meaning, purpose, and direction that employees crave in times of uncertainty.

Chapter Three

My Human Being Trumps Your Employee: The Essential Role of Emotion

More than anything else today, followers believe they are part of a system, a process that lacks heart. If there is one thing a leader can do to connect with followers at a human, or better still a spiritual level, it is to become engaged with them fully, to share experiences and emotions, and to set aside the processes of leadership we have learned by rote.

Lance Secretan

In the summer of 2008, a mid-sized manufacturing company was in crisis. Three weeks after being let go by the company, a former employee killed himself. A married man in his mid-thirties with two children, he had been a poor performer and troublemaker at the company. He was not particularly well liked by his colleagues, but when word came out about his death individual memories were pushed aside by shock, disbelief, and confusion. Chief among the emotional and mental reactions to the situation was the unmistakable fact that he had taken his life so soon after being fired. Very quickly, a widespread feeling developed among the employees that the company had caused the suicide.

The management team had felt secure in their decision to dismiss the problematic employee. Company leaders had spent an extended period of time managing his behaviour and had attempted a series of well-documented interventions designed to help him live up to expectations. As the tension grew following his death, management were forced to decide how they would deal with the situation. Ultimately, led by a manager new to his position but promoted from within, the team decided not to say anything to the staff about the incident. No meetings were held. No written or oral communication of any kind occurred. Nothing was done. Management's primary concern appeared to be that employees would blame them for the death, and they were keen to distance themselves from the incident. As the silence grew, employees concluded that management did not care, were afraid to face them, or felt guilty about what had happened. All these suspicions magnified the distance between workers and leaders, and intensified the crisis. The silence also left workers feeling that they were not supported.

As time passed, pressure on the management team to offer some kind of contact or communication increased. Ultimately unable to avoid doing something, the lead manager, overwhelmed by the pressures of a crisis so early in his tenure, arranged for a member of the company's human resources (HR) department to meet with the employees. When the time arrived for the meeting, the manager went on vacation. Disoriented by the events and lacking a structure to support them in coping with their feelings, employees were left to stew in their emotional confusion. This disconnect increased the distance between the managers and workers, leaving everyone, including the management team, feeling upset and hurt by what had happened. A climate of distrust and animosity emerged in the plant.

The management team's approach was unfortunate, though it was not surprising. In the face of personal fears and concerns, they put their heads in the sand and hoped that the issue would go away. This is a reaction I have seen many times. But the surprise here was that I was not only present for the whole event, I specifically advised the leaders not to proceed as they did.

In my meetings with the leadership team during the crisis, I worked hard to help them see that they were dealing with an issue of emotions. They needed to concentrate on the workers' feelings and overcome their own fears of being labelled responsible for the man's unfortunate actions. I advised them to talk to people one-on-one, to hold meetings before each shift, to let the workers talk about what had happened, and to illustrate that they cared about the employees, the dead man, and his bereft family, irrespective of his troubled work history. In particular, I remember a lengthy session where I mapped out for the new manager all the items he could communicate to his people in a meeting. He could convey that he was troubled by the news and concerned about the staff. He could explain that this was an important time for them to come together as a community. He could take questions and try to give accurate and fair answers. He could express that no one on the management team had seen this coming and that all the leaders were shocked by the news. He could explain that the details of the man's performance appraisals and eventual dismissal had to remain confidential, but that the decision to let him go was fair and followed a long process of support and correction. He could express his condolences to the man's family. He could explain that a fund was being set up to raise money to help the family. He could tell the workers that the management team and the HR staff would be available to support anyone who was having trouble coping with the news. He could offer to talk.

At the heart of my advice was the goal of connecting to people and helping them cope with their loss. I explained that by doing what I had advised, the manager would gain the respect of his staff. They would admire his courage for stepping forward and his candor in addressing the issues. They would appreciate the direct communication and see it as a model for coping with the situation. Starting the conversation would begin the healing and help people move on. His actions would improve the connection that his workers felt towards him, the other managers, and, ultimately, the company. More than anything else, a meeting would allow the employees to see him as a person who was as troubled by this event as they were. Seeing their boss grappling with emotion, including the sense of guilt that lingered around the event, would have given the entire team permission to acknowledge their feelings and resolve their conflicted loyalties. It would have made being human okay.

In the end, the manager was not able to take my advice. He and his team – employees and management alike – were left to cope with their emotions in isolation. Looking back on it, I have only sympathy for him and what he was going through. Having seen so many difficult and trying situations, I know that it is very hard to step forward and lead, especially in a case that positions you as a possible contributor. His reaction, while problematic and detrimental, actually gave him more in common with his employees than anything else. Why? It was an entirely emotional response. No matter where we are on the corporate ladder, no matter what our relationship to the events of a crisis, no matter how long we have worked in a setting or known the people involved, our responses to situations – especially crisis situations – are driven by our feelings. Had he been able to "stop and look fear in the face," as Eleanor Roosevelt famously advised, this manager could well have developed the "strength, courage and confidence" that comes from "doing the thing you cannot do." Instead, fear consumed him, and the opportunity to rise to a higher state of connection, belonging, and success – the opportunity to lead – was lost.

We Are Driven by Emotion

When working with organizational leaders, I often use the phrase "my human being trumps your employee." This language emphasizes that they are leading people, not units or items. The more leaders can focus on the humanity of their team and resist disconnecting from the group emotionally, the more successful – and efficient – the corporate recovery will be. When employees and their families feel connected to the team and the boss, they believe that their contribution and presence matter. Leaders who focus on the emotional needs of their employees, even when it means a delay to other operational considerations, contribute to their business recovery.

Dale Carnegie said, "When dealing with people, remember you are not dealing with creatures of logic, but creatures of emotion." Logic, rationality, and analysis are important elements of working and living, but the majority of our decisions – the ones we are aware of and the ones that brew mysteriously beneath our consciousness – are driven by emotion. Mary Helen Immordino-Yang of the Brain and Creativity Institute at the University of Southern California specializes in research on the role of emotion in thinking and learning. Using scientific studies of how the brain processes emotion, Immordino-Yang argues in an Association for Supervision and Curriculum Development (ASCD) article titled "Emotions, Social Relationships, and the Brain: Implications for the Classroom" that "it is close to biologically impossible for people to think without feeling, and vice versa … [B]rain studies reveal that thinking clearly is, in fact, an emotional process."[1] Stroke victims who have damage in brain areas connected to emotion make poor judgments in both daily social and high-risk situations, even though all other mental processes (what we might call reason or rationality) are functioning normally. This is because emotion guides learning, ethical judgment, and social awareness. Immordino-Yang emphasizes that even knowing whether we are on the right track in solving a math problem is determined by our emotions, though we think of math as purely logical.

Approximately three hundred years before neuroscience informed our modern understanding of emotion, British philosopher David Hume said that our "final moral conclusion depends on some internal sense or feeling that nature has made universal in the whole species." We can use our reason to outline possibilities, pros and cons, or implications of an action, but we are guided by emotion in choosing the best course to take.

The role of emotion in leading, learning, and making sound judgments in a post-crisis world cannot be ignored. If emotion is dismissed as weakness, errors in judgment abound, the recovery drags on, and divisiveness runs rampant, as it did with the blaming that took place in Toronto around the SARS crisis. Hospital staffers, the Chinese population, and the city of Toronto itself were labelled as responsible for the situation. A similar response to the tensions erupted in the wake of the 9/11 attacks, when residents of Lower

Manhattan felt that no one understood their plight. In both cases, the emotional turmoil lasted well after the high winds of the storm had died down.

All of us have the ability, to some degree, to understand other people's intentions, beliefs, and desires. If we put our minds to it, we are able to draw on our own experiences to predict another person's feelings, thoughts, and behaviours before they occur. We can combine what we know about other people with an awareness of our own feelings, thoughts, and behaviours in various situations. This skill is one of the essential capacities that a crisis leader needs to have, because it allows us as leaders to connect intellectually and emotionally with what others are going through. It will also lead us back, over and over again, to focus on the importance of emotion. Without this capacity, or the belief that it is important to monitor and connect to the emotional state of the employees, leaders can often miss the mark in their decisions about what employees need.

When I lead workshops on stress management, I hand out elastic bands and suggest that people stretch them to their full extent. While participants' knuckles are turning white against the resistance of the rubber, I ask them to look closely at what is happening. They report that the band is thinning and close to snapping. I then ask them to stretch it several times and see if it returns to normal. As they sit in the session holding their elastic bands, I suggest that elastics can be viewed as a metaphor for people dealing with a crisis or stressful situation. The more difficult the circumstance, the more it pulls at us. A degree of stress is manageable, but the opportunity to de-stress afterwards and return to a relaxed state is needed.

My point with this exercise is threefold. First, a crisis situation creates a period of prolonged stress in which there is very little opportunity to reset to normal. Second, stresses in one part of our lives have an effect on every part of the system, as seen in the way that isolated medical staff during the SARS quarantines became depressed based on what was happening in their work context. We are all a complete system: whatever happens in one context of our lives will have an impact on the other areas. Finally, the idea of being "stretched beyond the limit" is one to consider, not only for individuals but also for teams, departments, and entire organizations. Leaders need to figure out where the stresses are and who are being stretched beyond their limit as critical components of crisis recovery.

Our Emotional Needs in a Crisis

We Cope with Trauma and Grief in Stages

One of the most difficult things for leaders to accept is that a person's healing simply cannot be rushed, unlike various business practices, which can be accelerated under certain circumstances. Leaders who can adapt to this way of thinking and are committed to providing the caring and flexible circumstances required in a crisis are better suited to ensuring a full and healthy recovery of the people and the business. You just have to accept that you cannot rush the process.

Emotion in a crisis is somewhat predictable. When the event first occurs, there is a surge of adrenaline that sharpens focus and intensifies experience, but this phase of high-energy engagement is not sustainable. Eventually, as the days wear on and the new reality becomes normalized, people slip out of an overcharged state. At that point, they often slide into forms of depression. They feel a sense of weight, lethargy, and despair unlike anything they have experienced before. They are faced with the overwhelming task of trying to understand what has happened and to accept their new reality and all the significant changes that have occurred and cannot be undone.

There are many psychological models outlining the stages of coping with grief and trauma. But as a crisis leader, you don't need to have a strict handle on exactly what is happening with your people in a particular stage. You simply need to know that emotional healing is complicated and cannot happen at any other pace than the one the employee can handle. This perspective will help you when it comes time to make decisions about how and when you expect people to return to work.

We Catch Emotions from Each Other

During a crisis, sentiment spreads rapidly as a result of the heightened emotional state. Think back to people's reactions to blackouts that have occurred in Los Angeles and New York over the years. When the lights go out, law and order begin to erode, and rogue factions in various communities start to loot and pillage. Witnesses to the initial violations of the law soon became participants. The chaos grows. People who would not typically have violated the social order get involved, not because they are opportunists, but because the unsavory behaviour becomes a kind of contagion spreading through the group. Riots that explode around sporting events happen in a similar way, and are often unrelated to the outcome of a particular game. People in the streets get involved in acts of violence and disobedience based on the influence of others. The emotion spreads, and bedlam rises.

Workplaces are far from immune to this kind of emotional contagion. When a traumatic event occurs outside the building, in the boardroom, or on the plant floor, employees feel an immediate loss of control. If organizational leaders are not able to restore a sense of order and stability quickly, a company can end up with what I sometimes call a "panic parkway." As one person begins to show signs of fear, anger, or alarm, others follow suit. The momentum builds and slows the progress of recovery, leading to a series of adverse dynamics for the staff: acceptable workplace behaviour erodes, staffing problems increase, the ability to cover shifts falls, productivity and work completion rates decline, incidents of insubordination increase, employee health concerns grow, short- and long-term disability claims rise, more resignations occur, loyalty to the company diminishes, and the ability to recruit new workers is stifled. This "epidemic inside the epidemic" is ideally forestalled, or at least immediately addressed, if it arises.

I advise leadership teams to be proactive and assertive in addressing negative emotional trends on their teams. Nipping emotional contagion in the bud can help to keep it from spreading.

We Value Our Place in a Social and Cultural Group

The human need to belong is a powerful force that shapes our emotional reactions to what is happening around us. Organizations and companies are social groups; the more a leader can create a culture that represents the values and habits which support high functioning, the more success that leader will be able to achieve. The goal is to establish powerful cultural beliefs that are so embedded that everyone buys into them. One experience that illustrates our desire to fit into our cultural groups occurred in Istanbul during the earthquake recovery. I had quite a challenge on my hands. I had to quickly pull together a team of Turkish-speaking psychologists, social workers, and psychiatrists; facilitate transportation to Istanbul on short notice; and develop a disaster response plan that would integrate with a team of in-country Turkish mental health professionals assisting us in our efforts. As the only non–Turkish-speaking member of my contingent, I was at a distinct disadvantage.

Within hours of landing in the devastated nation, we were met by the local team hired by P&G, and we arranged an initial meeting to establish an action plan for the weeks ahead. Right away tension was evident in the room. I attempted to take the team through a first assessment of what we were dealing with and how we should proceed. But one of the in-country Turkish doctors, who was a P&G employee, constantly interrupted me, changed the subject, and tried to take control of the meeting. His actions made it abundantly clear that he was not interested in accepting my role in the recovery effort, even though everyone in the room understood why P&G had hired me. As the minutes passed the tension escalated, and I was working frantically inside my head to figure out how to resolve the conflict. I had been in power struggles before, but the complexities of the language barrier and this man's aggressive attitude made the situation difficult.

Just as I was considering some kind of dramatic gesture like adjourning the meeting, a solution presented itself. One of the men I had hired, a seventy-five-year-old Turkish-speaking psychiatrist from Montreal, gently lifted his hand in front of him and looked the resistant Turkish professional in the eye. When the local man stopped speaking, the older Canadian suggested that the two of them step into the hall. The meeting stopped, and they went out of the room, leaving the group of grown men and women sitting like school children waiting for the teacher to come in and resume the lesson. When they returned a few minutes later, the doctor who had been resistant to my leadership sat down, looked across the table at me, and, in front of his colleagues and the new group of Canadian experts with whom he would be working, issued a sincere apology for being disrespectful of my authority. I was stunned but covered my reaction and carried on.

What happened out there in the hall? That was the question I posed to the modest elder-statesman from Montreal when we returned to our residence to wrap up that first long day. He said, "I told him that his behaviour was an embarrassment to me as the elder in the room. Disrespecting an elder is inappropriate and unacceptable in the Turkish culture." It was a powerful reminder of the influence of cultural expectations.

We Need Contact with Each Other

Our pervasive need for human contact and connection was on full display in 2003 when I was involved in advising twelve hospitals in the Toronto area during the SARS outbreak. I offer a leadership profile from the SARS crisis later in this book, but the general effect of the outbreak on the population in Toronto helps to illustrate the impact of a crisis on people's needs. Thinking about what happens when a city is under siege by an epidemic clarifies why I have come to see belonging and relationships as the essential focus of crisis response.

SARS was a respiratory infection that came to Canada from China and had all the features of an epidemic you might see in a Hollywood blockbuster rather than at a hospital near you. The highly contagious virus was killing young and old alike, and the precautions required to contain it were unlike anything most people living in Toronto, or elsewhere, had ever seen. Because the disease was initially identified as an airborne infector, life changed rapidly for many, many people. Hospitals went into quarantine, staff were not permitted to go anywhere except back and forth from home, people inside and outside of hospitals started wearing surgical masks at all times, hospitals were closed to typical traffic, family members were not able to see each other, and a general level of fear permeated the city as the government and the hospital leadership worked to stop the spread of the disease. Initially, everyone was terrified that the disease was spreading through the community. But as the crisis wore on and the preventative measures began to take effect, the situation grew more complex. At this point, another widespread concern developed: alienation.

The precautions needed to prevent the spread of SARS meant that many people were separated from their loved ones, colleagues, and the general population. Far more taxing than the disruption of routines was the emotional strain of being denied access to the normal processes of life, which are the main sources of our connection to other people. In the hospitals I was advising, the leadership teams gave considerable thought to the problem of alienation, because the social and emotional tolls of the crisis were significant. The isolation created by the epidemic was incredibly stressful.

Imagine everyone suddenly wearing masks so that you could only see their eyes. Interacting without facial expressions is a gruelling way to live because it impedes our ability to care and connect. In addition, hugging, holding hands, or even patting someone's shoulder posed a risk, and the avoidance of physical contact added to the strong sense of isolation and loneliness that pervaded. For palliative patients, those coping with illnesses or complications due to surgery, or those dealing with intense life events like the premature birth of a child, this situation was very trying. For patients who were children, being asked to carry on without comfort in this masked reality was truly frightening. For hospital employees, basic approaches – like smiling to reassure a patient prior to giving a shot or placing a hand on someone's arm to indicate support – became impossible. Add to the list that normal forms of human connection were unsafe, such as getting a haircut or going out for dinner. Some people were housebound and could not get groceries. Others would not leave their homes because their neighbours were afraid of them. Everywhere, the stresses of isolation were evident.

The need for connection was revealed in the brilliant and creative solutions people crafted to solve the isolation problem. I remember a family that arranged a live video feed for a patient who could not attend a family wedding. I remember hearing about a mother who was sick in bed at one hospital and spent an entire night on the phone with her child who was also sick, but in another hospital. I also remember countless situations where the compassion and courage of the hospital staff led them into patients' rooms to just sit and talk. All these examples illustrate that offsetting isolation and loneliness was a priority. In every case, the healing power of human contact was on display.

We Fear the Unknown

John Kenneth Galbraith, the famous economist who advised the Kennedy administration, is known to have said, "All of the great leaders have had one characteristic in common: it was the willingness to confront unequivocally the major anxiety of their people in their time. This, and not much else, is the essence of leadership." Fear is one of our deepest and most primal emotions, and it is easy to see how fear was useful during the evolution of our species. When something threatening happens, every sense is sharpened. In a crisis, this fight-or-flight response helps us cope with real and present dangers such as a bomb, an earthquake, or a hurricane. Fear triggers a surge of hormones that support immediate reactions, and can be productive.

The fear that dominates during a recovery process is different. Once the routines of coping with life after an event take hold, people reflect on their situation, setting off a whole series of fears that are magnified versions of typical concerns. Under normal circumstances, people fear situations such as getting fired or reprimanded, a loss of security or stability, a change, or the unknown. During a crisis, these fears amplify. Anything leaders can do to dampen employee concerns is worthwhile, including a reassuring word, detailed information about a situation, or a compelling speech that illustrates the company's firm commitment to the recovery.

A crisis causes uncertainty and leads people to worry about what "normal" life will now look like. Catastrophes always begin with the unknown outweighing the known; the wider the impact of the event, the less certainty there can be. When the event is something like a plane crash, the list of unknowns is accessible but daunting: What happened? Why did it happen? Who was hurt? Could it have been avoided? Where are my friends, colleagues, and family? But in an event like the SARS crisis, where the causes of the epidemic are not known and the path to a solution is murky, fear grows and grows. In that case, because the early stages of the disease involved so many deaths – especially of young healthy people – the stress level was particularly high.

We Value Action

Every cultural tradition has standard practices for supporting people when they are grieving, partly because it is comforting to do things for each other. Even an act as simple as dropping off a meal for a neighbour following a death in the family is comforting to both the giver and the receiver.

In the wake of a crisis, this need for action is heightened, and there is a strong sense of purpose that ignites our bias towards action. This was evident during my earthquake experience in Turkey. I saw the power of taking action while witnessing two very different approaches, one from the P&G leadership and another from the Turkish government.

P&G had three manufacturing facilities in Istanbul, which employed several hundred people. Significant pressure was put on the leadership team to get those operations going again to avoid a loss of business both immediately and in the long term. All the employees were well aware of this priority, which is what made

P&G's approach to the crisis resonate even more deeply. P&G imme-diately took action to change the condition of its employees' lives. It secured shelter in the form of ground tents for survivors, spouses, and children. It opened its cafeterias and provided three meals a day for everyone connected to the company. It hired my team to help people cope with the emotional elements of the earthquake. And it provided supplies that the staff needed to rebuild their own homes. All these actions took place two weeks before the lights were turned on at any of the factories.

The effect of these decisions extended far beyond meeting basic needs. The actions spoke loudly to P&G employees, telling them in no uncertain terms, "You are the priority." These actions were well received because they were immediate and tangible.

By contrast, the Turkish government fell into a political quagmire. It made false promises about medical services and supplies, shel-ter, food, water, and support that left citizens feeling betrayed and alone. It resisted aid offered by other countries and left blood, medi-cal supplies, food, water, and tents sitting on ships docked in Mar-mora. Government officials talked at length about supporting and caring for their people, but their actions drowned out anything they attempted to communicate in words.

Our relationship to action affects how we experience the mes-sages of our leaders. People like to do things. The difficulty lies in finding a clear direction and purpose. This is where our need to be led comes in. When a leader can give a strong sense of purpose, provide a path for the organization to follow, and show employees how they can bring the vision to life, everyone feels called to action. Not knowing "what to do with oneself," especially in a crisis, is very stressful. We want to be valued, and we want to do something with our emotional and intellectual energy, but we often need help with how to do it.

This is why we value goals. Setting a target based on an idea and then working towards it is life affirming. Crisis situations illustrate that people's need for action is particularly evident in times of fear and anxiety. Having something useful to do helps people to cope.

We Have Trouble Seeing Invisible Losses

When a loss offers visible and tangible evidence, when we can experience the event directly through our senses, it is easier to believe that the loss is real. But losses that have intangible or indirect consequences are harder to grasp. When a child dies, family and friends have a palpable and direct experience to manage, and everyone participates in the grieving. When a young woman is told she is not able to have children, the news will generate a sense of loss, but it will be hidden from view. An outside observer might ask how a person can grieve something she never had, but the woman is dealing with a genuine, albeit invisible, loss. Yes, she can explore other options in order to build a family, but in the moment when the news hits her, something very real is taken away.

Depending on the nature of a particular incident, there can be evident and powerful outcomes. Destroyed buildings, loss of life, injured workers, and the widespread effects of a natural disaster can be seen and registered. But more personal and emotional losses tend to recede from view, and it can be easy to overlook the impact of the shock. For example, the 9/11 attacks dramatically eroded people's sense of security and confidence in the authorities charged with keeping them safe. In addition, the violent nature of the attacks left many people feeling a loss of innocence and hope. These are abstract concepts that are foundational to people's sense of security.

I saw a similar situation in the Cayman Islands. Workers recovering from the effects of a hurricane had a long list of visible damage to cope with, but their sense that they had lost paradise dominated their hearts and minds.

We Find Comfort in Group Membership

A significant risk in any organization is the development of a feeling of "us versus them" between the leadership team and the employees. Strong organizations regularly bridge this gap, and successful leaders keep people connected. In a crisis, the pressure to divide grows, but so does the importance of staying close.

When stressed, afraid, confused, or agitated, we gravitate towards the people we know. We seek the comfort of our compatriots and want to be with others who are like us. We want people who "speak our language." This need applies to both the workers and the management team. After all, isn't it true that people who gravitate to leadership roles have some things in common and can relate to each other? Even in organizations with a solid feeling of community prior to the crisis, new habits can emerge that separate people. This isolation leads to distrust and misunderstanding, and conflicts arise if no effort is made to invest time in reconnecting. In seeking the comfort and closeness of small groups, a feeling that "they don't understand us" can develop among employees, and the cohesion and sense of community in the wider organization may become threatened. In this way, our need to connect, which drives us to reach out to others in a time of stress, can also pull us away from people.

Sometimes, the corporate culture and the leadership's actions combine to actively widen the group-based divide in a company, with predictable consequences: animosity among the workers, damage to relationships, long-term scepticism about motivations and interests, and diminished loyalty to the business. Leaders who send out subtle, often non-verbal, messages that everyone is expected to just "get on with it" after the event create a barrier to unity and healing. Unrealistic expectations introduce stress, and I have seen situations where companies worked actively to pit departments and social groups against each other. They created peer pressure to return to work and leave the crisis behind. Their goal was to make returning to work and productivity a competition, with winners and losers based on employees' willingness to ignore or override their own feelings. In all these circumstances, an unfair environment forced people to feel guilty about the emotional obstacles they were facing.

In general, I find that employees want to work hard and support both the company and their colleagues. Being pointed out as someone struggling to pull their weight adds unnecessary and counterproductive strain during a recovery.

Appreciating the tendency to cluster into familiar and like-minded groups is important for leaders during a crisis. The leadership team must be proactive and outgoing about making connections between people and creating a sense of community throughout the entire organization. They should hold as many large group meetings as possible, and produce a constant stream of communication that focuses on the shared goals of the entire team. It is also important to see the value of shared experiences outside of normal work contexts. Whatever technique is used, resisting the tendency to divide will improve the overall health of the organization.

We Are Damaged by Negativity and Bullying

Another side effect of crisis is that negativity can run rampant. As the stress level increases, people develop animosity towards each other. They fall into blame in the face of confusion, guilt, shame, fear, and loss. Add this to the tendency for emotions to spread quickly in the workplace, and there is a high risk that past efforts to build community connections will be undone. In particular, I have seen many situations where one or two people had a substantial negative effect on a large group. I call these people "toxic tornados."

When a person spreads antagonism and resistance, other people often fall in with the complaining and criticism. We all need to belong, and most people would rather join a group of disgruntled colleagues than stand on their own and express a balanced view of the leadership. It's a bit like a snowball rolling down a hill: whether the snow is clean or dirty, it is going to get picked up by the growing mass.

A crisis can also magnify a pre-existing condition of maltreatment between co-workers. A company with a "bully" runs a huge risk that this conduct will spin out of control following an incident. Bullying is highly concerning and can be difficult to pinpoint. But the effect in a workplace is the same as it is on students who have to endure this kind of treatment: victims grow sheepish, hesitant, and withdrawn, and often blame themselves for what is happening. Left unchecked, bullying creates a hostile and unsettling climate.

It would be hard for me to overstate how essential it is for leaders to confront and address bullies and toxic tornados. In my experience, addressing this behaviour is one of the most important responsibilities of leading during a crisis, and doing so will have an immediate positive impact on the atmosphere and employees' view of the leadership. Just as insubordination is still insubordination in a time of war, a crisis is not an excuse for poor behaviour. In fact, I would say that during a crisis there ought to be a higher standard for civility, patience, and a forgiving attitude. Professional conduct simply has to be non-negotiable, and harsh criticism, offensive language, and rude behaviour have to be unacceptable.

I advise organizations to have well-written policies about professional conduct as a framework for interventions. To avoid the spread of negativity and reduce the harmful effects of bullying, there can be no delay in putting a stop to damaging behaviours. Workers will appreciate swift action, feel like the barre is set for their conduct, and rise to the occasion. At heart, people are ready and willing to support the overall efforts of the company. Sometimes they just need help getting out of a difficult situation that only the leadership can address. The emotional climate among workers can alter the organizational culture in a hurry. Even companies that have been strong and vibrant prior to an event find it very difficult to maintain a positive and cohesive team during the aftershocks.

I was in this position myself in New York City in 2001 following 9/11. While the counsellors were busy with the workers we were supporting, I was handling all the dynamics and logistics of the operation. From coordinating with company leaders to arranging transportation for our team, I had my hands full. Each morning, after only a few hours of sleep, we would meet to talk about the day ahead, hand out the assignments, and design our approach. In the first two days, one of the counsellors stood out. He was loud and rude with everyone he spoke to and complained constantly about the assignments he received. He also grew more and more angry as the work progressed, and began to take his anger out on anyone who came into his line of fire. Late in the first day, I had a very direct and pointed conversation with him about his conduct. I gave him specific details about how his approach was affecting others, and directed him about how he could change it. At the end of the second day, it was evident that he was not able or willing to change, and I was obliged to put him on a plane that night. It was a hard conversation to have, but the impact on the team was palpable and immediate. He simply needed to go.

Techniques for Supporting Emotional Needs

Eighteen years ago, I was working for a large national corporation, and the owner of the firm was reckless with the company's money, spending on homes and vacation properties, cars and travel, restaurants and entertainment. His approach was fine when the company was flush. But when we were not able to make payroll for our more than four hundred employees and associates, many of whom were my direct reports, the financial model became harmful. Soon after the birth of my second child, I learned that I was not going to receive my paycheque. My wife Janet was on maternity leave, and I was suddenly in a situation where I could not cover our monthly expenses. In a panic and not really sure what to do, I drove downtown to see my immediate boss, Tom Reynolds, at his home. I respected Tom, and I had the sense I could ask for his advice.

Tom welcomed me into his home, and we got right to the topic at hand. To my surprise, I learned that Tom had not been paid either. Then the most stunning thing happened. As we sat in his living room, Tom pulled out his personal chequebook and wrote a cheque to cover my salary for the month. I remember being grateful and overwhelmed. I have never forgotten the sense of loyalty my family and I felt towards Tom, and he and I have been close friends ever since. He is also one of the first leaders I came across who illustrated the critical importance of directly addressing people's emotional needs.

Live Among Your People

The primary advice I give leaders during a crisis is to spend time with their people. The more face-to-face contact they can generate, the better. Simply being in the same space as someone has a huge effect on that person's sense of safety, security, and connection.

I encourage leaders to park in the employee lot, eat at the company cafeteria, greet workers as they come into the building, and use the same washrooms as the employees – anything to increase the level of informal contact. It is also critical to be on site almost all the time. You may be concerned for your own safety, physically or emotionally exhausted, or faced with your family wanting you at home. But whenever possible, you need to remain at work. Not only is this essential in order to create regular contact with employees, it is critical for demonstrating that you are committed to the crisis recovery and appreciate everyone's contribution. Workers keep track of when the boss comes and goes. Use this scrutiny for the benefit of the team.

I was reminded recently of what this principle looks like in action when I was waiting for a flight at the Ottawa airport and stopped at a roadhouse restaurant to get some dinner. As I made my way to a table, I saw a man seated at the bar who looked familiar. After a moment, I realized it was David Miller, the former mayor of Toronto. Seeing him instantly reminded me of the one and only time I had met him in person.

Roughly ten years earlier, I had received one of those eerie calls in the middle of the night to respond to an incident. A crew at the Toronto Transit Commission (TTC) was working in the middle of the night to remove asbestos from the walls along the track when there was a significant accident that killed one worker and injured two others. Emergency medical services (EMS) workers had attended to the victims, and my contact at the TTC had asked me to provide trauma support to the other members of the crew. I headed to the TTC rail yard, expecting to find a handful of track workers and a few supporting staff members. But I came across a scene I had not expected: Mayor Miller in a baseball cap and sweatshirt talking to the group of affected employees who had formed a circle with him. The mayor had come straight there to be with these employees in the first moments of the crisis.

Remembering the incident prompted me to re-introduce myself to the mayor. After reminding him of how we knew each other, I asked him what he had had in mind that night in the TTC yard. He thought about my question for a minute, and then simply said, "I think that as a leader, you have a responsibility to be present."

Recognize Specific Actions Immediately

One of my mentors, Dr Steve Stokl, used to say about recognition that "grown men die for it and babies cry for it." Leaders need to give far more credit than they take; acknowledging workers is never more important than during a crisis. "Catch them doing great" is a phrase that my former colleague Dr Ed Miller of the Montreal Children's Hospital uses to emphasize the importance of sincere, informal, and natural opportunities to celebrate successes. Recognizing effort both publicly and privately creates a culture where people feel valued. Even a simple acknowledgment in front of a co-worker is powerful.

Make positive feedback constant and immediate. There is no time like the present to comment on the good things happening in your organization. Recognizing contributions right away ensures that informal feedback will actually happen. If you wait until you are back in your office, you will likely lose track of a mental note to send an email or follow up. Walk up to someone and tell them they did something well, and be as precise as possible. Vague phrases such as "good job there" or "you're doing great" feel wooden and rote, and suggest that you may not know or appreciate the person's role in the company. Be specific. Point out to a custodian how clean and tidy the office looks despite the power disruptions, or recognize the willingness of a line worker to extend a shift or work through a break to support a colleague or a company goal. Real recognition has real content.

I also advise leaders to avoid falling into the trap of recognizing people based on position. Pointing to anyone who has done outstanding things – irrespective of job title – is an important way of saying that you value remarkable effort. Sincere and accurate comments are appreciated by everyone. I counsel leaders to give credit to their staff in all contexts, which includes ensuring that all public relations interactions are focused on the efforts of the team. Whenever you speak to the media, point out all the ways that "we" have pulled together to deal with the adversity. The more leaders can take the spotlight off themselves and put it on the efforts and successes of the workers, the healthier the culture and the more effective the recovery will be. You should also celebrate the successes of departmental teams and units to increase team pride and develop a sense of community.

Whatever you can do to create forums for sincere and ongoing feedback will help. Artificial and forced forms of recognition put people off and create distance. Moreover, if you are seen to be recognizing your workers only because there has been pressure to do so, your efforts will fall flat. This happened during the SARS crisis when there was a general silence from the political leadership in Toronto and Ontario about the efforts of the healthcare workers to cope with the epidemic. Only when the world started to react with a series of pseudo-economic sanctions in the form of advice not to travel to or do business in Toronto did the government step forward and exclaim how incredible the hospital employees had been. It was too late for positive comments to be taken as heartfelt. Recognition needs to happen early and often.

Know People's Names

Knowing names is a leadership technique that every good school principal understands. It is also one of the easiest ways to determine if a leader cares about the people on his team. When we use people's names, we tell them that they are valued and relevant. It is a simple but powerful act. Long before a crisis occurs, leaders need to learn the names and stories of the people on their team. I know it can be difficult in large organizations, but the benefit is significant.

Using people's names also ensures they receive your message, because they pay closer attention and take what is being said more seriously if they feel that you know them.

I was once asked to go into an industrial work site after a horrific accident had resulted in the violent death of a long-time employee. As it happened, the deceased had mentored many of the new employees over the years as they learned the ins and outs of the business. He was a popular and respected member of the team. The CEO of the company, who had also been mentored by this man, had a remarkable skill for remembering names. He had thousands of frontline employees, and I witnessed him regularly mention workers by name in casual conversation. For days after the incident, he spent hours walking the plant floor, standing at the assembly line, and referring to anyone he could talk to by their name. I was stunned by his ability, and, to this day, I believe that his commitment to knowing people was one of the primary drivers of their efficient business recovery.

A recent experience further emphasizes the power of using names. I was teaching a group of air traffic controllers in Winnipeg, Manitoba, about crisis incident response, and the topic of personalizing relationships came up. At a break, a gentleman named Patrick approached me to share a life-changing experience.

He had been a football player in high school and was recruited to play for McGill University, my alma mater. Shortly after preseason training camp began, Patrick injured his neck quite badly in a collision with another player and ended up at one of the local hospitals. While he was lying on a gurney outside the imaging department with his neck immobilized and staring at the ceiling, he realized there was a person sitting at the foot of his bed. This person was evidently a recognizable figure, because everyone who passed by said hello. In time, the individual stood above Patrick, looked into his face, and inquired about his condition. To Patrick's shock, it was the former prime minister of Canada, Pierre Elliott Trudeau. The two men talked, Mr Trudeau wished Patrick well, and then left.

Four years later, when Patrick was walking through the Roddick Gates at McGill, he looked down the street and saw Pierre Trudeau walking towards him. As they drew nearer, Trudeau said, "Patrick, how are you? You must be close to graduation." The two spoke briefly, and then the former national leader went on his way, leaving Patrick feeling like a king.

Avoid Unnecessary Top-Down Decisions

There are dozens of decisions to be made during a crisis, and I have seen many leadership teams centralize authority and rely on the efficiency provided by small groups. This practice is a trap to avoid. People feel empowered and valued when they are involved in decisions. A leader who imposes decisions rather than solicits opinion and input alienates employees and slows the recovery process. Allowing an emphasis on time efficiency to distract from the core idea that a crisis response is a shared event will damage the corporate culture during and after the rebuild. Involving people builds a solid foundation of trust and engagement with long-term effects.

The key is to look at a decision and be careful not to conclude that it is "essential" and must be made quickly. In my experience, there is often more time to consult with the team than it may appear. In addition, imposing decisions on people runs the risk of decreasing your own effectiveness. Lack of input from the people who will be executing a given policy or living out the implications of a decision creates the risk that your plan simply will not work. The risk is especially high in large corporations, where the senior management can be quite removed from the frontlines. Always remember that the right side of the leadership equation – the direction – has to be non-negotiable. If you give your people a destination and then leave them to work out how they will travel the path, you will simultaneously engage them and create the conditions for ideal solutions.

Limit the Amount of Change

A crisis forces a re-evaluation of change management. From projects that were in the works prior to the event to changes required by the crisis, the number of potential changes can be overwhelming. Remember that people already have a huge amount on their plate just coping with their own emotions. If you load procedural and organizational changes on their shoulders, their level of stress will rise, and you will dampen the effect of the recovery. Leaders are often people who thrive in a state of constant change. They need to remember that most frontline workers find change difficult and stressful. Add to this that there will be numerous changes in response to the crisis – such as infection control measures in the face of an epidemic – and the prospect of new initiatives requires careful evaluation.

Rudy Giuliani remaining mayor of New York during the recovery process was a brilliant way of ensuring continuity as people coped with the event. A similar effect occurred when Jim MacLean, CEO of Markham Stouffville Hospital, shut down the emergency department so that his people could focus on managing the patients they had and not have to cope with new arrivals. Stabilizing the institution and insulating against an onslaught of change is an important way to support people and build trust.

Keep Track of Ripple Effects

Much like throwing a stone into a pond, a crisis has a point of emotional impact, after which the shockwaves travel out in concentric circles to people beyond the event. For example, in a manufacturing site explosion, people are killed or injured in the blast at the centre of the event. Shockwaves hit employees who witnessed the explosion and travel outward to employees who work at the site but were not on shift or in the building at the time. Moving further outward, shockwaves emanating from the event also affect those who work at other locations or have retired but are still part of the corporate community. All these different groups of employees have families, who become further circles touched by the event. If the event is covered in the local or national news, it will also have an emotional effect on people who were not previously connected to the company.

Assessing and being realistic about the emotional impact of a crisis helps you to accurately predict, prepare for, and respond to the needs of the people involved.

Monitor Your Own Emotional State

A leader's capacity for understanding and reflecting on his or her own emotional state in a crisis is critical. Self-awareness ensures that you can honestly and effectively interact with everyone in your care, and establish a connection to the emotional state of the employees and families you are looking after.

If the general manager of an industrial plant, on the job for more than twenty years, has just lost a long-standing employee to an industrial accident, that manager has experienced a significant loss that will take time to process and needs to ask, "How has this death affected me?"

When Lyne Wilson was locked down in the NAV CANADA head office after the 2014 shootings on Parliament Hill in Ottawa that left a Canadian soldier dead, her husband and daughters were at home, and she was not able to join them. By tuning into her experience and reaching out to others through her stress about being separated from her family, Lyne was able to use her own experiences to enhance the care she provided for her team.

LEADERSHIP SUMMARY

Key Concept
• The more leaders can focus on the humanity of their team and resist disconnecting from the group emotionally, the more successful – and efficient – the corporate recovery will be.

Emotional Reactions in a Crisis
• We cope with trauma and grief in stages.
• We catch emotion from each other.

- We value our place in social and cultural groups.
- We need contact with each other.
- We fear the unknown.
- We value action.
- We have trouble seeing invisible losses.
- We find comfort in group membership.
- We are damaged by negativity and bullying.

Techniques
- *Live among your people*: be on site at all times and find formal and informal ways to connect personally with employees, such as where you park, eat, and socialize.
- *Recognize specific actions immediately*: acknowledge employees' efforts in person and right away, ideally in front of others, and avoid praise based on position.
- *Know people's names*: take the time – long before the crisis – to know people enough that you remember their names and something about them.
- *Avoid top-down decisions*: wherever possible, include employees in decision-making processes and give them clear objectives and the flexibility to sort out how those goals can be achieved.
- *Limit the amount of change*: revisit initiatives and projects that were in place before the crisis and be careful about how quickly you bring them back online so that your people can focus their energy on the recovery process.
- *Keep track of ripple effects to peripheral groups*: extend your crisis response efforts to groups beyond the core employees to create a healthy community.
- *Monitor your own emotional state*: be mindful of how you are feeling and allow yourself to go through all of the stages of reaction to the event.

Chapter Four

Calm and Connected: The Importance of Continuous Communication

Precision of communication is important, more important than ever, in our era of hair trigger balance, when a false or misunderstood word may create as much disaster as a sudden thoughtless act.

James Thurber

When engineer Tom Harding walked away from the crude oil–laden train under his care, he could not have known what was going to happen. It was 11:25 p.m. on 6 July 2013 in Nantes, Quebec. Harding had followed company protocol, setting both the air and mechanical brakes on five locomotives and ten tank cars, and leaving the lead engine running to power the system. He then took a cab to L'Eau Berge hotel in nearby Lac-Mégantic, commenting to the driver that the situation made him uncomfortable. The engine was not running properly and had to be left on a main line because the side tracks were occupied. Minutes after he left, a fire broke out on the locomotive, and Harding did not know about it. Nor did he know about the disastrous series of events that had begun and would permanently change thousands of lives, including his own.

Details of the accident at Lac-Mégantic as reported in the media are well known. At 11:30 p.m., a citizen near the train saw the fire onboard and called 911. Arriving on the scene, Nantes's firefighters followed standard procedure and shut down the locomotive to eliminate the risk that its fuel would explode before putting out the fire. They contacted a rail dispatcher in Farnham, Quebec, who worked for Montreal, Maine and Atlantic Rail (MMA), and track repair workers were sent to the site. The workers assessed the scene, staying on site after the firefighters had left, and ensured that the train was secure before heading off for the night. They left the locomotive, which they could not restart, unable to supply power to the air brakes. Close to 1 a.m., secured only by the ten hand brakes that Tom Harding had applied, the train, which had been left at the top of an incline, began to roll down towards the town of Lac-Mégantic. Crewless, it hurtled onto an intricate section of track where it derailed, creating a wave of fire that killed dozens people and burned entire blocks of the town to the ground. This event was the largest rail accident in Canadian history.

Almost immediately, lines of communication lit up. First responders coordinated their efforts, cell phones and computer screens across the world reported news of the crash, government agencies worked to establish a plan of action, and citizens of Lac-Mégantic scrambled for answers: What had happened? Who was hurt? Are we safe? Who is going to help us? Where will I sleep tonight? Somewhere in the centre of it all, Tom Harding was coordinating with volunteers and firefighters to remove the nine freight cars that remained intact. As information spread like the fires that consumed the town, MMA management was not seen assessing the scene in town or up in Nantes.

I am not a public relations expert, and media relations is not the focus of this book, but a brief look at the reaction to MMA's handling of communications with the general public and Lac-Mégantic is instructive. CEO Edward Burkhardt was criticized for arriving on the scene forty-eight hours after the accident, and his company was almost entirely silent during that period. As *Financial Post* reporter Nicolas Van Praet wrote two days after the incident, company officials were "crucified mercilessly" on television and on the Internet: "So what started as the story of an inexplicable tragedy morphed into a narrative of a foreign company unwilling or unable to share in the communal grief."[1] When he did arrive, Burkhardt's press conference and interactions were handled so poorly that the CBC ran a story with the headline "Railway Head's Lac-Mégantic Visit Panned by PR Experts."[2] Seemingly unprepared and untrained, Burkhardt came across as haphazard. He also stated that he believed "the train engineer" had failed to set the brakes properly. As the face of the company's response, Burkhardt's approach was inconsistent with the basic principles of crisis communication, projecting an image of indifference about the needs of Lac-Mégantic citizens and seemingly insensitive to Tom Harding, who was just beginning to cope with what had occurred on his watch.

Why did the company's ineffective communication strike such a chord? Why did its silence and inaction cause so much outrage and criticism that it became "the story"? How can communication be so important? The answers lie in the idea that crisis communication is, in essence, about relationships. It is as much, maybe even more, about helping people – especially the employees – cope with events as it is about keeping them informed.

I refer to communication as the "lifeblood" of an organization, because it connects distinct units. The emotional turmoil and intensity of a crisis create a strong desire for information from the leadership. Your success in managing a recovery hinges on how well you handle communication. Everything you say and do sends messages to both employees and outsiders; everything you don't say or don't do communicates even more. Uncertainty and upset create a deep need for security and calm, and people look to the boss for this reassurance.

When I train executive teams, I use an activity called "seeing eye partner" to illustrate the relationship between trusting communication and successful outcomes. I create a maze and let all the participants see it in its entirety. I then ask people to pair up, and have one of the partners put on a blindfold. The seeing participant is responsible for verbally guiding his or her partner through the maze without contact, using only three instructions: stop/go, left/right, take x number of steps. Invariably, the more accurate the instructions and the more patient the guiding partner, the more confidently the blindfolded partner proceeds through the maze. Efficiency in completing the task is a direct result of the quality of the communication.

When I debrief the activity, participants who were blindfolded talk almost exclusively about how the directing partner's tone and clarity were helpful to them. As Stephen Covey writes, "When trust is high, we communicate easily, effortlessly, instantaneously … [W]hen trust is low, communication is exhausting, time consuming, ineffective, and inordinately difficult."[3] I try to help business leaders see this line of logic: trust leads to effective communication, and effective communication leads to successful outcomes.

It can be hard to convince corporate leaders that communication with their employees involves more than information and messaging. The pressures to address resource issues, the multiple demands on their time, and the spectre of the bottom line often drive leaders back to a preconception that emotional concerns are peripheral. They think it's *nice* to consider feelings if you have time, but nowhere near important enough to emphasize emotions during a crisis. Some leaders believe that the road to crisis recovery is paved with dollar signs rather than cleared by engaged and energized employees. Other leaders perceive communication as a kind of war, with secrets to be kept, a message to "manage," and a story to "control." It is hard for them to accept that communication is, in and of itself, the point.

The tone, frequency, forum, and tenor of interactions affect employees' well-being. In time, with gentle but constant insistence, many bosses come to see things differently, but it takes a commitment to rethink conceptions about what information is and why people need it.

Why We Need to Know

Cognitive neuroscience is a relatively new field of study that is generating a great deal of insight about the human brain. Combined with tangible experience, these insights create the opportunity to expand how we think about communication, because they help to fill in why people act as they do.

Dr David Rock, co-founder and CEO of the NeuroLeadership Institute, a global consulting firm that brings scientists and leadership development experts together, has written about the way our brains interact with information. In his essay "SCARF: a Brain-Based Model for Collaborating With and Influencing Others," Rock explains, "Much of our motivation driving social behavior is governed by an overarching organizing principle of minimizing threat and maximizing reward."[4] He illustrates that the brain craves certainty because it is a "pattern-recognition machine that is constantly trying to predict the near future."[5] If there is a level of uncertainty about the future, Rock says, we cannot concentrate on anything else. The uncertainty consumes us. He outlines that any kind of significant change (such as occurs in a crisis) creates massive stress for people. In times of instability, we look for ways to establish regularity and predictability in our daily lives so that we can face the days ahead. Anticipation is a major part of our thinking.

David DiSalvo, science writer and author of *What Makes Your Brain Happy and Why You Should Do the Opposite*, echoes these ideas:

> Years of neuroscience research have led to the current understanding of the brain as a prediction machine – an amazingly complex organ that processes information to determine what's coming next. Specifically, the brain specializes in pattern detection and recognition, anticipation of threats and narrative (storytelling). The brain lives on a preferred diet of stability, certainty and consistency, and perceives unpredictability, uncertainty and instability as threats to its survival – which is, in effect, our survival.[6]

DiSalvo categorizes many features of our mental lives that shape our reactions to information and communication. Here are three that I have witnessed in times of crisis:

1. *Certainty bias*: a tendency to perceive increasing levels of ambiguity as greater levels of danger: "The brain doesn't merely prefer certainty over ambiguity – it craves it. Our need to be right is actually a need to 'feel' right."[7]
2. *Selectivity bias*: a "tendency to orient oneself toward and process information from only one part of our environment to the exclusion of other parts, no matter how obvious those parts may be."[8]

3. *Availability bias*: "A happy brain tends to make judgments using the most accessible and available information."[9]

Rock and DiSalvo illustrate why and how we seek stability and security, sometimes called "cognitive closure," in uncertain times. I have seen this need on display again and again during periods of great stress.

Our Communication Needs in a Crisis

We Need Information

If you think about a typical day in your organization, you will realize that there are hundreds of conversations taking place at all levels, on all topics, at all times. We cannot exist in a community, or in our lives, without conversation and interaction. This inescapable fact creates a demand for information that drives us to know. People talk and talk, discussing topics from the weather to political news to neighbourhood gossip. It's just what we do.

When a crisis turns up the emotional heat, the need for information and communication increases exponentially. Without a steady stream of information from the leadership, people will seek easily accessible content and often end up in conversational dynamics that are harmful to the work environment. Here is the availability bias at work: the closest information at hand becomes the most powerful. This need for available information drives what I call "breaking news addiction," where people are so desperate for the latest piece of information they flock to anyone who is able to offer something. This undermines trust in management, adds to workplace anxiety, and promotes negativity.

We Cannot Accept Inconsistencies

People often respond to shocking and disturbing news by prying into inconsistencies they perceive in the story. It is normal for people to pursue additional information or explanations to understand the circumstances of a loved one's death, for example. People will also actively test the messages they hear from the leadership if there are things that don't make sense, and the employees' trust in the boss will be influenced by what they find out. If any part of the story does not fit with their conception of what has or could have happened, they will attempt to explain the disconnect, because the incomplete story is unsettling. Ignoring unresolved inconsistencies is nearly impossible. Our need for certainty and cognitive closure underlie the stress of not having available and coherent information.

We Tell Stories

Listen closely the next time you pass a group of workers or managers talking. I'll bet you will hear someone telling a story. As a Maritimer, I know first-hand about people's deep need to tell tales – and sometimes tall tales. I also know that any good story requires a full commitment to the art of narrative – not just the facts – and that people often inadvertently alter the details of a situation as their story unfolds. In my work, I have seen how the compelling nature of an incident increases the impulse for storytelling. Crises are inherently high drama events, and stories of risk, outrage, immorality, conflict, and animosity make "good telling," with their truth content sometimes a secondary consideration. This process can cause a chain reaction of information modification that generates new so-called "truths."

We Don't Like to Say "I Don't Know"

In the 1950s, Art Linkletter hosted a show called *Kids Say the Darndest Things*. The premise was that the host would ask kids grown-up questions and see what they said. Something comical like this would happen: "What is habeas corpus? Oh, that is the white vegetable Mom makes me eat." What Art and his producers knew is that kids will not say "I don't know." They will make something up.

Guess what? Adults do it, too. Rumour, gossip, and hearsay flow from our need to fill in the blanks. We don't want people to think we don't have information. As DiSalvo pointed out above, we don't "feel right" not knowing something, so we speculate and guess. Our need for information, our preference for certainty, and our aversion to ambiguity create a climate where the accuracy of information circulating through the organization can decline rapidly.

We Love Simple Answers

Stereotypes and oversimplifications take root because our search for certainty and need for cognitive closure drives us to settle on an answer as quickly as possible. Our need to feel confident in our beliefs or decisions is so significant that our brains are only "happy" when we can confirm what we are already thinking. This quality leads to the classic "us versus them" narrative about the relationship between management and workers. Visit the local movie theatre, and you will see that we love stories about good guys and bad guys. Casting the boss, the employees, the organization, or the government in the role of villain is an age-old hobby.

We Trade Information

Our need for news and certainty means that "information is power," leading to the inevitable creation of a market for information. I have seen dozens of situations where competition for information is intense, and workers try to outdo each other to be the one who has the "scoop." The result is that unverified information spreads, and the rumour mill becomes the source of truth. Information trading also leads to a sense of mistrust towards management, because people tend not to focus on the accuracy of rumours. Instead, they focus on the fact that they did not hear the story from management. This kind of "malignant messenger" effect is injurious to the overall climate of trust and community that companies work hard to establish.

We Accept Perceptions

Our brain's selectivity bias is behind the age-old phenomenon that perceptions become reality. We all have conceptions about people, events, and organizations from our daily experience, and our brains want to confirm what we believe. We tend not to be sceptical about quick conclusions. We look for evidence that can confirm our pre-existing hypotheses. These biases were on display in one situation I saw, where the leader had to hold back on paying salaries based on a reasoned assessment of the long-term needs of the company. He was immediately viewed as cheap, despite making a decision that was judicious under the circumstances and led the firm to be able to retain as many employees as possible.

We Process Emotions Out Loud

Regardless of your attitude towards counselling sessions, keep in mind that people mainly process emotions through language. From group therapy to nightly conversations between spouses, the preferred mode of venting, recapping, or just plain feeling is through talk. Some people are inwardly oriented and don't express much at work, waiting for more private moments, but others are wired to talk about whatever is on their mind whenever they have an opportunity. When this happens in a crisis, the endless loop of rehashing all available information – for anyone who is willing to listen – creates a kind of emotional spiral that gets everyone riled up.

We Need to Get Along with Others

Being part of a group is incredibly important to people. The need to be accepted and liked and the desire to avoid conflict run deep. People are not necessarily – or ever – going to derail a "bitch session" in an effort to offer a balanced perspective on the subject at hand. The energy and force of the moral outrage often accompanying gossip or misinformation is so powerful that even the most principled employee will struggle to put a stop to a conversation. The employee might opt to avoid those people, but that won't stop the flood of negativity washing over the organization. Looking to employees to solve the problem within their own social group is unfair and ineffective.

We Need to Connect

The ubiquity of social media is evidence enough that our need for relationships drives us into constant contact with others. Yet, despite an endless stream of tweets, blogs, and emails, we all have a deep need for live contact. There are enormous benefits, including a sense of calm and connection, to in-person interactions. The more live contact people can have with each other, especially in times of upset and agitation, the better they will feel. The tone in people's voices or the look in their eyes helps us feel that there are people in the world we can connect to who are like us.

Techniques for Meeting Your People's Communication Needs

A close friend worked for an international conglomerate that had been one of the largest global leaders in its industry and had a well-established reputation for excellence. The company was often viewed as the benchmark against which all other companies were measured, and sales representatives from rival companies were regularly asked about this big firm's products rather than their own.

When I spoke with my friend, the firm had begun a substantial financial decline, its reputation plummeting relative to many upstart companies in the field. It had fallen into bankruptcy protection, was struggling to secure new investment, and was hemorrhaging long-standing clients to the competition.

While the firm was fighting for its life, the management team's approach was to close their doors to staff, ignore any and all questions, leave the office regularly without an explanation, offer pat and superficial answers if they were ever pinned down in an elevator or hallway, and issue a few email updates to their employees. Predict-ably, rumours sprang up, staff and client anxiety grew, and office productivity plummeted.

As its performance fell and clients elected to cut ties with the firm, the top representatives in the sales force were recruited by rivals and began taking their books of business elsewhere. The peak of this exo-dus, and the flashpoint event that stood out in my friend's mind, was the departure of the global number-one sales representative and her multimillion dollar accounts. Four business days after this rain-maker resigned, the management team members were still seques-tered in their offices. They made no effort to contact the remaining employees, and gave the impression that they viewed all questions and concerns gossip that ought to be ignored. Not a single executive spoke to the employees: there were no individual conversations and no small group meetings, full staff meetings, emails, or letters.

A counterpoint to this example already mentioned is Rudy Giuliani, who demonstrates how effectively a leader can connect to people when he makes himself available. Giuliani's response to the 9/11 attacks was a force in the success of the recovery. When I was in Man-hattan, I never met him or saw him in person, but I felt like I had. He was ever-present in the newspapers, electronic media, and daily con-versations of citizens, which created the reassuring sense that some-one was always there. There was never a doubt that he was in charge, and his confidence and resilience were a symbol of New Yorkers' col-lective will to overcome adversity. His impact stretched well beyond the Hudson River, as he became a national figure who personified the American spirit. Being present in the streets, hospitals, homes, and funeral gatherings became his signature. He left the running of the city in competent hands and went out to be with the people. Giuliani is a model for the kind of relationship-focused leadership I advocate.

Plan Your Communication Processes in Advance

Communication during a crisis is a fine art that requires talent and resources. You have to be solid in yourself as a leader and need a pre-existing rapport with your workers. You also have to be committed to a collaborative recovery, ready to wade into uncertainty or confusion, and talk – *really* talk – with people.

This commitment requires a plan, because a gift for the gab will not solve all the issues that come up. Communication goals need to be grounded in the knowledge of what people need, which means focusing on the emotional climate rather than emphasizing the logistics and tactics of getting operations back online. Establish security, trust, safety, and calm to ensure a unified approach and a speedy return to productivity. Crises bring uncertainty, and people feel off balance and lost. Set the tone, and remind the community that everything will get better.

Create a culture of trust and openness before a crisis occurs to set up the right relationship between the leadership team and the employees. Starting this process in the middle of a recovery is nearly impossible. After setting the tone, ensure that all appropriate policies are in place, establish the communications infrastructure needed to manage high-speed interactions, get proper training for all leaders, and allocate time at regular intervals to make sure that all systems and processes are in place before a storm hits. This last one can be hard, I know. Leaders are under immense time pressures every day, and the thought of making time to talk about something that may never happen seems a stretch. All I can say is this: if the odds of a crisis are as low as you think, there wouldn't be so many gainfully employed crisis response consultants.

Be the Reliable and Predictable Source of All News

The first thing I emphasize with leaders is the need for speed, clarity, and consistency of internal communication with employees – a process that is related to but entirely separate from any outside public relations efforts your organization engages in. You are in an arms race to become the source of information, up against the various social media and mobile technologies, the lightning-quick mechanisms of gossip and rumour, and the dozens of ways that a message can get garbled even when it has been communicated effectively. Do everything possible to provide your people with information that will shut down alternative sources.

Structurally, an organization needs a command centre that can be set up right away in an accessible location. Right from the start, provide direction about where to give and receive information. Then make sure your team can keep up with the supply and demand for news. Lapses into silence or infrequent updates will lose the audience and begin an almost unwinnable war against misinformation and confusion. No matter what else you are dealing with, make sure you have an internal 24/7 news channel open and running, even if sometimes all you report is that you have nothing to report. The act of communication is as important as the facts of communication.

After establishing your own internal version of CNN, publish a schedule of times and places for meetings, and stick to it as much as possible. Regular updates create a degree of calm, because anticipating the meetings will ease some of the craving for information. Try to hold meetings at least once a day, increasing the frequency if events and developments warrant it. Decide on a spokesperson for the group, and, whenever possible, have the same person do all the communicating. It is ideal if this person is the most senior executive, but that may not be possible. Just remember: it is not a good idea to offer a member of the HR department. No matter how talented and articulate your HR staffers are, workers need you or an acceptable surrogate leader. The point is to foster an emotional connection to the boss and the organization, not to provide well-packaged facts and details.

At the meetings, provide information that matches what people are hearing elsewhere. Inconsistencies will lead to speculation and mistrust, resulting in rumours and fabrications that are nearly impossible to undo. Once bent, setting the record straight is very difficult.

In terms of content, think through your priorities, but don't plan the message too carefully. Your goal is to share as much as you can, and if you ever wonder whether you should disclose something, err on the side of more. In particular, discuss the latest findings, decisions made inside and outside the organization, successes and areas of complication, and any changes in direction since the last communication. At all costs, avoid circumstances where information leaks out in advance or someone in a leadership role has an "off the record" conversation. The meetings need to be a sacred occasion where information comes to light. Call impromptu meetings if there is breaking news of some kind. Waiting for the next scheduled meeting is not always the best bet, especially with difficult news like the confirmed death of a colleague. Tell them what you know – right away. If you are managing a large organization, ensure consistent information right down to the departmental level so frontline workers can interpret the situation in ways that make sense for them. Remember to keep middle managers informed, give everyone opportunities to ask questions, and make communication as open and consistent as possible.

Make Live Meetings a Priority

You'll notice I have not said anything about the quality of the emails you write or the blog postings you offer. I know that those forums can be relevant, especially in situations that involve the media and the world beyond your organization, but when dealing with your own people, always talk to them live. I appreciate how hard this can be. Events, physical distance, and time constraints can make it nearly impossible. You have to try, even when it means dealing with multiple shifts, because every employee needs to feel valued. This can be challenging when dealing with numerous times and locations, but do all that you can. People cannot cope with emotion while staring at a computer screen or a smartphone. They need to hear your voice and directly experience your sincerity and intensity. You can only be an emotional anchor if you show up in person. No matter how hard the meeting is or how much negative feeling has built up between workers and leadership, have the courage to sit with your workers, or stand up in front of them, and talk.

Live meetings are also essential because the content of the message will invariably play second fiddle to the tone those interactions take. People respond to sound or manner even more than to words. Communication is a kind of crucible where your commitment to the community will be tested. More than any other time, a crisis pushes leaders to demonstrate they care. Talk is important, but, as Ralph Waldo Emerson writes, "[W]hat you do speaks so loudly, I cannot hear what you say." Throughout the recovery, how you act, where you are, what you are doing, when you come and go, who you spend time with, and all other behaviours have expressive power. It's like that moment when a person you are walking with stops to pick up a piece of garbage before carrying on down the street. Nothing is said, but you learn a lot about that person's character and values.

I am talking about the power of multimodal communication. "What you say is only the beginning," says Harvard Business School (HBS) professor David Thomas, quoted in Deborah Blagg and Susan Young's HBS article "What Makes a Good Leader?" "Your behavior, your actions, and your decisions are also ways of communicating, and leaders have to learn how to create a consistent message through all of these."[10] Think of this as an amazing opportunity. Model a respectful, calm, accurate, open, and confident approach, and you will galvanize your teams' determination. Be professional but informal. The goal is to reassure and engage people. Reading from a script or responding stiffly to questions won't do. Make some notes and follow them, but speak in your normal voice. Don't be afraid to pause to breathe or reflect, especially if intense emotion is involved. The more you can let yourself be a person to the employees – within the bounds of professionalism and appropriate distance – the more they will feel valued and connected.

Have a system in place to send an electronic communication and a hard copy of everything discussed, including questions and answers, after every meeting. A quickly generated record of the content reaches out to anyone not in attendance, giving them tangible evidence that they are valued equally with those who were in the room. Hard copies also give everyone present an opportunity to read over the content again: most people struggle to take in everything they hear. Assume they are walking away with only part of the content. This kind of attention to detail reinforces the idea that you are on top of the communication and that they can count on the systems you have established.

As far as other technologies are concerned, using the phone or a video link is fine if you cannot establish a live meeting, but they are not ideal. That said, these technologies are a step up from email or letters as the initial contact. I advise companies to put in their pre-crisis policy documents that "electronic communication will support personal contact" and not the other way around.

Value Openness and Equality

If I say "be honest with your employees," you might find it condescending. It isn't. Honesty is one of the most important and most challenging aspects of effective communication. If you don't know something, say so, and say when you think you might, making sure you circle back when you said you would. If there has been an error, admit it. If you have some information but not all, say so. And give your information in as unfiltered and unpolished a fashion as you can. Authenticity is compelling. The more you come across as human, the better – faults, fumbles, fidgeting, and all. The more straightforward you are, the more likely it is that when employees compare everything you say with what they are hearing elsewhere, it will all "make sense" in their minds and add to their confidence in your integrity. This approach is especially important if the leadership team's goals are not particularly popular. If you publish your goals and are open about your intentions, trust will be maintained. There is a difference between disagreeing with the leadership and understanding that they are acting in the best interests of the company. In my experience, people know that leaders have tough decisions to make; they just want to understand what is going on.

Jim MacLean, CEO of Markham Stouffville Hospital north of Toronto, was brilliant at this. I have a vivid memory of him standing in the intensive care unit (ICU), masked, gowned, and gloved, during a meeting in the throes of the SARS epidemic and talking openly with everyone. The tenor of the meeting illustrated that people were onside, because they sensed that Jim was giving them the "straight goods." As an alternate example, the neonatal intensive care unit (NICU) leadership at the Hospital for Sick Children did not have a reputation for candor when faced with a crisis, and this lack hampered their ability to maintain a good relationship with their staff. This is why it's important to create a culture of openness well in advance. No matter how honest your communication during the recovery process, memories of distance and silence will persist.

Much of what I am advising here is about "transparency," the dreaded "T" word that has become so hackneyed. The problem is that the idea is right. As in the "seeing eye partner" activity, people will proceed confidently if they have a solid sense of where things are headed and why. It will also improve their loyalty on a long-term basis, establishing the sense of community you want. The irony is that the term "transparency" has lost its meaning as a result of the ineffective and cold communication of some corporate leaders. Claims about "transparency," coupled with secrets revealed later, have created a distrust of the term.

Because of the critical need for trust and confidence, I am very firm with my clients about their behaviour behind closed doors. How the management thinks, talks, and feels about the employees will influence all their interactions. If bad mouthing the "workies" is acceptable, that attitude will infect the workplace. It's also highly likely that word will get out. Even members of the management team have a tendency to love the "mean boss" narrative. Information will leak that the bosses look down their noses at the common folk, undermining every sincere expression of concern from the management team. No matter what you say after that, employees will "hear" you referring to them as "the idiots who work here."

Brilliant leaders do not walk around thinking they are superior to their employees. They know that their skills have positioned them at the head of the organization, but they don't conceive of themselves as more important than anyone else. Their commitment to equity shows in every interaction they have, from talking with the cleaners on the night shift to talking to the chair of the board. Great leaders see themselves as working "for" the employees, not the other way around, and they are open about this attitude.

Be Open to Input and Listen

No matter how many briefings you lead, never assume that you are getting it right or that you cannot improve your approach. Even if you are a seasoned public speaker, debrief with people who have an ear for effective communication and who will tell you honestly what they think.

Quoted in Blagg and Young's HBS article on good leaders referenced above, Nitin Nohria, dean of the HBS, maintains that "communication is the real work of leadership" and that great leaders are able to make any message accessible, no matter the listener's background.[11] Nohria's colleague John Kotter also emphasizes this idea: "Great communicators … understand the people they're trying to reach and what they can and can't hear. They send their message through an open door rather than trying to push it through a wall."[12] Consider a parent who stands close to a young child and gently tosses a ball instead of throwing it. The goal is to make the "pitch" so that the child can make the "catch." The same is true of communication, which must be guided by the needs of the listeners and not the expertise of the speaker – though of course, that expertise informs the exchange.

Along similar lines is a phrase I picked up when I was invited to speak about functional communication to a group of hostage negotiation experts with the Ontario Provincial Police: "Talk so they will listen and listen so they will talk." Their negotiators' experience in a high-stakes context where miscommunication can have immediate and dangerous consequences gave me a whole new appreciation for the value of straightforward expression. It also reminded me about the critical importance of effective listening.

Dale Carnegie devoted much of his mega-selling book, *How to Win Friends and Influence People*, to the importance of listening, and there is widespread agreement in leadership literature that leaders need to be highly effective listeners.[13] Patiently and fully listen to questions and give the best answers you can muster. Remember that you are not speaking solely to convey information; you are there to reassure, connect, and convey your acknowledgment of others' needs. One person asking a question represents at least ten people with the same concern. Leaders who think that communication is only about information transfer get frustrated when similar questions are asked over and over. Leaders who understand that the process is about coping with emotion and supporting each person make as much time as possible.

Share Information, Ideas, and Input

In addition to direct communication, I advise organizations to encourage the sharing of information and ideas among their teams. Positive interactions between groups are an antidote to isolation. Begin by empowering people. Whenever employees come forward to point out a problem in the organization, charge them with finding a solution, and let them be the ones to tell people about it. Then, begin to promote widespread conversations about how things are going. Positive, supportive, and collegial interactions unify the team and feed the sense of community. Groups can talk about the information received at meetings, but they should be advised to identify successes and concerns as well. I also promote sharing between facilities and businesses – especially in situations that affect multiple organizations. The more open discussion you can generate, the more you can save time, conserve energy, and get people focused on the recovery.

During the SARS epidemic, silos existed at all levels as groups, including departments, professional groups, corporate leaders, and entire hospitals, isolated themselves from each other. These separations added enormous tension to an already divisive situation.

My work during the SARS epidemic was a time when I saw the use of a very effective solution to interdepartmental distance and tension. A few months after the crisis, I was working with North York General Hospital to support its rejuvenation efforts when I received a call from one of the leaders about an unspoken yet significant conflict between the emergency department and one of the medical floors. Tension between the employees was causing a bottleneck in patient and information flow. As I looked into the situation, I spoke to each department, inquired about their impressions of the other people, and heard over and over again that these two groups of people had never met in person. I was somewhat shocked, but it led to an idea. The staff on the medical floor hosted a breakfast for the emergency department and even arranged for a staffer to dress as a clown and deliver invitations right in the emergency room (ER). At the breakfast party conversations ensued, and new relationships began. After that, the bottleneck in the workflow was cleared, and relations between the two departments were much smoother, partly as a result of the efforts of Tim Rutledge and Karyn Popovich, the leaders who led the way to a solution.

Deal with Negativity and Misinformation Immediately

My advice thus far has been focused on creating a positive climate in your organization, but I know there will inevitably be a degree of negativity and misinformation, usually in the form of rumours and gossip. No matter how hard you try to centralize the communication and connect to everyone, some people will derail your efforts, even if they don't intend to do damage. You have to be ready for this reality.

Long before a crisis ever occurs, create a written "no gossip" policy in your HR manual and your emergency response plan so you can use these documents as management tools when the time comes. Then be proactive and assertive in addressing negativity. Establish a conduit for information about what is happening on the frontlines, namely staff who will keep you informed about misinformation travelling around – not because they want to be spies but because they believe in the importance of a unified positive approach. If you hear about widespread misinformation, address it immediately. The longer you wait to set the record straight, the more difficult it will be to convince people of the truth. Be direct with employees who are spreading inaccuracies. Give them an outlet for information, and encourage them to work with you in maintaining the integrity of the team. Even the simple act of approaching someone to inquire "How do you know this is true?" and "What is the source of your information?" can influence that person to make better choices and join the effort.

LEADERSHIP SUMMARY

Key Concept
- Communication is the lifeblood of business recovery, because it is the primary means for connecting with your employees. You need to ensure that you constantly, consistently, and positively communicate with your people.

Communication Needs in a Crisis
- We need information.
- We cannot accept inconsistencies.
- We tell stories.
- We don't like to say "I don't know."
- We love simple answers.
- We trade information.
- We accept perceptions.
- We process emotion out loud.
- We need to get along with others.
- We need to connect to people.

Techniques
- *Prepare your communication processes in advance*: establish a pre-existing rapport with your employees that creates a culture of

trust and closeness, and then set up communication goals and plans that focus on their emotional and social needs.

- *Be the reliable and predictable source of all news*: make sure that people hear all important news from you, and communicate on a regular schedule, even if all you do is tell them you have nothing to tell them.
- *Make live meetings a priority*: people cannot process emotion behind a screen or on the end of a phone call – they need direct contact with the leadership so they can hear your tone, see your body language, and feel your presence.
- *Value openness and equity*: be yourself as much as possible – stammering and all – and never badmouth the employees in any setting so they can relate to you and trust you.
- *Be open to input and listen*: ask for and integrate feedback about your communications.
- *Share information, ideas, and input*: ensure you listen, involve employees in problem solving, and encourage them to work together with other departments to solve pressing problems.
- *Deal immediately with negativity and misinformation*: talk right away with anyone who is being harmful or spreading gossip or inaccurate news.

Part Two

The Stages of Crisis Response

Chapter Five

Four Leadership Profiles

You cannot create experience. You must undergo it.

Albert Camus

Profile #1: Procter & Gamble and Hurricane Katrina

Hurricane Katrina, one of the worst natural disasters in the United States, hit the Gulf Coast on 29 August 2005. It mainly affected Alabama and Louisiana, and caused devastating damage in the city of New Orleans.

In November 2005, I had the opportunity to interview Tom Spedding at the global head office of Procter & Gamble in Cincinnati, Ohio.[1] At the time of Katrina, Tom was director of human resources: global disaster management. I had worked with Tom in Istanbul to support P&G through the 1999 earthquake, and he had previously managed another large-scale disaster during the 1995 earthquake response in Kobe, Japan.

Procter & Gamble is a multinational consumer goods company best known for products such as Tide, Folgers coffee, and Crest toothpaste. The company's explicit purpose is to be an ethical corporate citizen and to improve the lives of its customers.

When Tom and I talked about his experience overseeing the response to Katrina, I was hearing from an expert in the field. Having been through two major crises before, Tom and P&G had a wealth of experience they could draw on. His wisdom helped him see what the real priorities are in a crisis, and he was able to clearly articulate the link between immediate responses and the long-term effects of the company's approach.

> I think the company needs to always look at the long haul. Yes, you have to do some things that are expedient in the moment, but we mostly try to make decisions that are going to sustain the enterprise long term. I think crisis response is a good example of something you do where you have to make decisions in the moment, but a lot of what you do is going to be remembered for a long time. You invest in your people, and you might not get a return right away, but the approach will pay dividends long term. For example, when you invest in employee health and well-being, it can be hard to justify some of the expenditures up front, and the benefits come with time. You build goodwill with the employees and their families and the community, and it has a lasting effect. But it can be hard to measure. We expect a lot of our employees as far as their performance and their commitment to the company goes, so we have to expect a lot of ourselves. We have to show them examples of the leadership doing the same thing. In a crisis, we do the right thing for people because it is the right thing to do, but also because it makes good sense from a business perspective: it builds trust and loyalty, which are key to success.

P&G's corporate policy sets the needs of the employees first. Tom's view represents P&G's position that the success of individuals and groups is central to the overall success of the company. In the case of Katrina, this commitment to people was evident, given the significant damage and potential loss of business that occurred because of the storm.

> We have our Folgers coffee plant in New Orleans, which is the coffee plant that supplies all of North America. It is a very strategic location for us. The hurricane hit early Monday morning around 4 a.m., which was around thirty hours ahead of the eye of the storm coming

to the area. Our plant is in Slidell, Louisiana, which is an area that was in the news quite a lot because it sustained major damage from winds and flooding. It is a plant that runs twenty-four hours a day, seven days continuous operation. After the storm, about 60 per cent of our employees either lost their homes entirely or had them damaged to the point that they were uninhabitable. The storm had a massive impact on our people and our operations there.

Tom's focus was on the hurricane's effect on P&G's people. When he outlined the major initiatives taken in the wake of the storm, he demonstrated that the company's emphasis had been on helping people get back on their feet – not just because it was the ethical thing to do, but because it was the best way to maintain the well-established operational efficiencies of the plant. It was the prudent fiscal decision.

When we were first working to make contact with the employees after the hurricane, there was a risk that a person might not hear from us and might conclude that the plant was shut down and they needed to look for work elsewhere. It was important for us to reassure people that we would be getting the plant up and running, and that there would be work for them. If we had not worked quickly to connect to employees and provide support for them, I think there would have been a breakdown in trust, and people would have begun to consider leaving the state. The devastation could easily have led people to conclude they should move to a place like Texas, where flooding is not an issue. By connecting to our people and showing them that we were there for them, they stayed with us, and that helped to get us back to 100 per cent productive capacity and get them back to their full pay as soon as possible. We ensured our business continuity by taking care of our people. If we had had to recruit and retrain new employees, it would have been very difficult, and it would have had an effect on the perceptions of Folgers in the local community.

P&G's sensitivity to the ways in which people perceive the company and its commitment to behave in an ethical fashion were a driving force in the positive reputation the company has in the New Orleans community and elsewhere around the world. They are also a key part of P&G's competitive edge.

> People expect that we are going to respond in a humane, professional way because we expect them to do the same thing when they work for us. We emphasize the importance of being responsible, and if we were not that way toward our people, the community would have lost confidence in us. It has to do with reputation management, and it extends beyond the community to the media. When news is instant and you have a global company like Procter & Gamble, stories would spread quickly through the state and the nation if we were not taking care of our people. So it's the right thing to do, but it is also helpful for people's perceptions of the company. I mean, President Bush chose to come to our plant and tour when he came to New Orleans, and he talked about P&G as an example of a company that is in the community for the long haul and about how we might be down but we are not out. The result was that it kind of showed other corporations that if they want to compete with P&G, they will have to do more than just produce a good product. They will have to compete for the feelings of employees and for a reputation like P&G has for being a wonderful company to work for. P&G kind of pushed them all to hold their own feet to the fire.

Tom was also very clear about the importance of doing things properly. Disaster relief is a very expensive proposition, but providing the needed funds for employees is the best path to profitability in a crisis. In particular, Tom explained how P&G's approach to recruiting from within benefited the company and showed the ways in which this commitment amplifies the importance of taking care of your people.

> You know, if we had done things on the cheap, we might still not be up and running, because our employees would still be dealing with where to live and how to take care of their families. And their families

might not be saying, "P&G is a great company." They might be saying, "Look, Dad, I want you to leave and find work somewhere else." Procter & Gamble is a promote-from-within company, so our system is dependent on employee loyalty and continuity – having people stay with the company. We don't bring people in to plug holes. If we lose a plant manager, we don't just hire from another company. We grow them from the bottom up, and we work really hard not to have much turnover, so we don't lose people we have developed and groomed. We try to give people expanded responsibilities or new opportunities that will keep them here. Workers who we are recruiting know this about P&G and want to work for us because we take care of our people. It is part of our PVP: purpose, values, and principles. We have been emphasizing that idea with our people for a long time, that the business and the employees are inseparable. Treat others like you would like to be treated. If the company is going to be sustainable and profitable, the employees have to know that you are being supportive.

P&G is a massive corporation with operations all over the world, but of all the organizations I have worked with, P&G has one of the most humane and sensitive approaches to disaster response I have ever seen. It has built a culture where people matter more than anything else, and it follows that commitment through in every crisis that it faces.

Profile #2: North York General Hospital and SARS

In 2003, Canada was hit hard by SARS, a highly contagious respiratory illness spread through close contact with an infected person. It is reported that there were 438 cases of SARS in Canada, including 44 deaths.[2] The disease was very difficult to contain, and healthcare workers in particular were at risk of contracting it.

. On 10 December 2005, I sat down with Bonnie Adamson, CEO of North York General Hospital (NYGH) during the SARS epidemic.[3] I worked with her and her senior team on site during the epidemic.

NYGH is a teaching hospital located in the north-central area of Toronto and affiliated with the University of Toronto.

The SARS crisis was an enormous medical and public health challenge for everyone involved because of the nature of the illness. Bonnie had spent her entire career working in healthcare, moving up from shift nurse to the top job, and was really clear about the unique nature of this disease.

> SARS was an unknown lethal virulent disease that silently infiltrated this organization and attacked our staff, made them sick, attacked patients, and shut down operations. It was kind of like a movie. All of a sudden you realize that all around your environment, internally and externally, there is this huge crisis that no one can diagnose and no can treat with confidence because it had never been seen before. Survival becomes your focus: survival of your people and patients, and survival of your organization.

Among the multiple issues that Bonnie and her team had to cope with during the crisis was the speed of onset. There was no warning that the disease was coming, and no one knew how serious it was going to be. SARS created one of those crises where the leadership and the entire population of the hospital, city, and province were scrambling to get ahead of the situation right from the start.

> The crisis situation across Toronto had emerged almost overnight, and NYGH, like the other hospitals, was rapidly responding. When SARS I began, we had an increasing census [number of patients] in the hospital as a whole, because other hospitals around us were shutting down their operations due to the number of SARS patients in their organizations. Our emergency department, obstetrical area, and operating rooms were working at more than full capacity to deal with patients from other organizations in addition to our regular patients. On a board in the command centre, we constantly tracked the morning census, night census, number/categories of SARS patients, and the total volume of patients by program, creating the "big" picture at a glance.

Changes in these indicators of activity were happening quickly, plus staffing and operational issues were emerging constantly. That was March. That was SARS I. We peaked at thirty SARS patients, and as quickly as humanly possible our staff were converting rooms and wards with negative pressure systems to best isolate patients. All the while, directives in rapid succession from the Ministry of Health were being studied and implemented across the hospital. As a large team of leaders, we were using our collective leadership/management expertise and background experience to lead the hospital at this difficult time. As CEO, I also kept the board of directors' chair informed twice daily because of the acuity and risk of the situation.

Bonnie and her team had massive resource issues to deal with while they tried to keep everyone safe. But what made this particular crisis so difficult was that SARS came in two waves, creating a false sense of calm after the first phase of the disease, while also giving the hospital leadership some small opportunities to learn from their earlier experiences.

As the month wore on, the census was climbing because we were receiving patients from other nearby hospitals where the operations were shut down due to the SARS patient activity. For example, we delivered one hundred more births than the normal activity, and the emergency department was overextended most of the time. Therefore, our volumes kept rising higher than normal. At the same time, we were finishing the construction and opening a new building. Our staff worked on the weekend to be sure to get the areas open as quickly as possible, and we paid construction workers extra money to be sure their work was finished as soon as possible. The board of directors was proactively informed of all these decisions. It was a chaotic time that continued until around mid-April. Public health officials declared that it was over. Little did we know what was ahead.

After SARS I had passed, and we were in the process of trying to review our response to strengthen our crisis response and risk management protocols, SARS II hit on 23 May and another nightmare began.

All of a sudden, a major crisis had hit NYGH once again. During the second phase of the disease, we put 7,000 people in quarantine for fourteen days, and the entire time we were in a continuous crisis.

Leading a major medical centre is a complex task, and Bonnie was continually faced with existing issues in the organization, which became significant problems as the leadership team attempted to deal with the needs of the patients and staff in the face of SARS. For example, she had to navigate the long history of union–management relations and find a way to bring people together in the common cause of coping with the crisis.

> One major issue early in the command centre activity was about union membership at the command centre meetings. Like many hospitals, the history of the relationship between management and unions reflected distinct and separate worlds. The unions wanted a seat at the command centre decision-making table, and the management approach was not to include them. A strong attitude existed about "that's union and that's management." I thought about my extensive work with unions over time and my learning that if you bring them in and help solve problems early, they know when they are in conflict and when to leave. From experience, I believed that if you involve them in decision making wherever possible, they own the decision and it is easier to implement. However, that was not the culture at the time, and I could not change the dominant attitude in the moment. I decided not to fight that battle at that time. On reflection, if I was in the situation again, I would have intervened and allowed them to participate. It may have made things easier for the organization as the time went on. We had no idea what was ahead of us.

In my experiences with Bonnie, both talking with her and also seeing her in action, I learned that she approaches leadership with an emphasis on what is right for people. When the crisis was over, Bonnie was celebrated for her work leading the hospital through the crisis, but she was also enormously successful in transforming the culture of NYGH into a thriving and collaborative work environ-ment. She is a leader who loves her job, loves working with people, and wants to be at the heart of things.

> The entire crisis was a time when we had to rely on core leadership qualities. These included strong listening, empathy, and sensitivity to the politics of the scenario, both inside and outside of the hospital. It was really important to watch everything happening around you very attentively. I would go home at night exhausted but totally exhilarated. In the morning, just like the other leaders, I could not get to work fast enough. We needed to be there as much as humanly possible because visibility of leaders was important. As CEO, I made rounds regularly and often with senior medical staff to areas where SARS patients were being cared for and other areas.

Profile #3: Nova Scotia Power and Hurricane Juan

Hurricane Juan hit Nova Scotia, Canada, on 29 September 2003. It knocked over trees and brought down power lines, leaving more than 100,000 people in Nova Scotia without power for several days. The hurricane caused about one hundred million dollars in damage and was blamed for eight deaths.[4]

On 17 April 2006, I sat down in Halifax with Nancy Tower, vice-president of Nova Scotia Power (NSP) during Hurricane Juan.[5] NSP is a privately owned utility regulated by the provincial government, which is located in Halifax and provides electricity to about half a million customers. Juan was a unique event in that the winds and storm were a significant issue in and of themselves, but the after-effects were the most troubling – in particular, the state of the power grid and all related lines and poles.

> It was October of 2003. The actual hurricane hit on 28 September, and we fought the storm for the week that followed. Luckily, hurricanes blow through fairly quickly, so the event itself was over in a matter of hours and that allowed us to get out on the road, because the winds

had died down by the middle of the night. We were able to get people out there to begin the restoration effort.

Power companies like NSP have well-established protocols for coping with storms and outages, but Juan was a whole new experience, with a level of disruption and damage the company had not seen before, because the power transmission to a huge percentage of its customers was disrupted.

In a normal outage, the control centre gets the call, and they dispatch by calling the supervisor who is on standby and waking them up in the middle of the night to go and deal with the situation. Our staff deal with the outage, and they often have to deal with the weather, but not at the level that was required in this situation. The weather was a huge factor. But we were also dealing with the sheer volume of customers whose power was out. I remember watching the needle on the gauge of the power that was going out of our generating plants going down like a car running out of gas. There was so little power demanded that we had to back off the power being generated. The damage was so widespread that we had issues with the stability of the entire electricity system in Nova Scotia – the kind of issues that you just don't deal with during normal power outages. This outage was on a whole different level than the typical situations we had dealt with in the past.

This situation was also different because it happened at night. People sometimes make bad decisions, so in some ways we were lucky that the hurricane hit in the middle of the night. If people were out during the storm watching it all, they would have been at huge risk. If the hurricane had happened in the middle of the day on the Sunday, people certainly would have been out watching it – in places like the Point Pleasant Park. People would have been at risk of being hit by falling trees or the storm surge. Overall the damage was enormous. I remember driving home in the morning from the control centre to try and get a bit of sleep before going back. I could not believe the devastation. You had to pick your way through the streets because some of the streets were simply impassable. It was just unbelievable.

Huge trees knocked down. I remember thinking, "Oh my God," and looking around trying to take it all in. Huge trees on streets like Young Avenue and Oakland Road. Just unbelievable.

On the Sunday evening and as the storm began to intensify, the emergency measures organization and the local and provincial governments declared a state of emergency so they could evacuate people. Early in the evening and because of the high winds, we were experiencing some power outages, what we call feeder distribution outages, where the power is out to a number of homes because a tree branch hits and takes the power out in an area. So we had trucks with crew and supervisors out there dealing with that. But as the storm intensified, so did the number of customers without power.

One of the critical lessons that Nancy drew from the experience was the role of a leader in a crisis and how much there is to track and manage. As we talked, she emphasized key principles that a leader has to keep in mind.

You have to be there all the time with your ears open. That was an important lesson I learned. You cannot be absent. If you are in a crisis situation, you've got to be there both physically and mentally. And being calm under pressure is so important. Making decisions with your head and supporting your team. If your team makes a decision, you have to support them. You need a good team of strong people who can make decisions, and you have to let go and let them lead. And then be calm in the situation so you can all move from one decision to the next. Those are key skills you need to have.

Nancy was very clear about the critical elements of an effective response and the ways that NSP followed through in the face of the crisis as everyone involved rose to the challenge – guided by the leadership team.

We talk about Hurricane Juan as a defining moment for the company because we called on literally everyone in the company to participate.

Even our CEO was in the call centre with a headset on, answering calls along with a number of our senior executives. And some of the senior executives were out knocking on doors to help with the community liaison program. We worked together in the hardest hit areas because without power there is no TV or radio, so it is tough to get the message out. The way that people experience a crisis is a big part of how you are viewed as a leader. You have to communicate effectively. Our main goal was always simple and non-negotiable: get the power back on. But keeping customers informed is really important for the relationships and success of the company over the long term.

It took fourteen days to complete the restoration, and the call centre was running 24/7. We had to ask people from all over the organization to get involved. As our CEO says, we pulled together and through brute force got it done. We all pitched in to help. We were very proud of what we were able to accomplish in that time. We surveyed our customers afterwards, and people felt that Nova Scotia Power did a great job responding to Hurricane Juan. I think people could look outside and see why their power was not on. People were very understanding. They could see us doing our job, and they were thankful. So when the power came back on, everyone felt we had done a good job. But most of all, Juan brought the whole company together as a team. Even my smaller group – the emergency operations centre team, my head of T&B [Thomas & Betts] assets, and my head of regional operations, the head of the control centre, the senior directors – the whole team bonded over it. We worked hard and we made good decisions.

While all their recovery efforts were underway, Nancy and her team knew that there were certain principles at the heart of the recovery effort that simply had to be maintained – especially as they related to the health and welfare of the employees. NSP's approach to taking care of its people while attempting to ensure a speedy recovery was evident.

Our objective is always to get the power back on as quickly as possible to the extent that we can in the face of foul weather, and our customers certainly expected that of us. We have a strong safety culture, and we are working towards becoming a world-class safety organization, so the safety of our employees is number one. We will not compromise the safety of our employees.

Profile #4: NAV CANADA and a Triple Homicide of Three RCMP Officers

On 4 June 2014 in Moncton, New Brunswick, Justin Bourque shot five RCMP officers, killing three and severely wounding two. A terrifying thirty-hour manhunt required a lockdown in the Moncton subdivision of Pinehurst, where several employees and families of NAV CANADA lived. NAV CANADA is a private company that owns and operates Canada's civil air navigation service, and is the world's second-largest air navigation service by traffic volume.

On 4 June at approximately 11 p.m., Lyne Wilson, director of human resources and employee relations for NAV CANADA, called me to ask that the Tibbo & Associates disaster team be on standby to assist her in ensuring that NAV CANADA staff and their families were cared for during the crisis. I have worked with Lyne and NAV CANADA for over ten years, and soon after our phone call that night, Lyne and I got down to work.

When the crisis was over, Lyne and I communicated over the phone and email to debrief the process we used to support the NAV CANADA employees.[6] This profile is illustrative of the kind of crisis response processes that can be used by large organizations but on a smaller scale in the face of an event that has affected a particular subset of their community.

We had approximately twenty employees plus their family members in the locked-down area in Moncton. The CISM [critical incident stress management] team from Moncton requested assistance, as they felt more help was required than what they could offer, given the sheer numbers but also given the fact that they were affected by the events themselves. At the time the decision was made to send a team, the lockdown was still ongoing, and we did not know if we would have any employee or family member killed or injured. In order to be prepared for the worst, an emergency team was put together within twenty-four hours to be able to respond to the Moncton employees and family members.

Lyne and her team were particularly fluid in coping with the crisis, and were able to provide and alter available resources in response to the shifting needs of the situation. Their focus was on providing support to their employees that would allow the employees to cope and heal in the most authentic and accessible fashion possible.

In the early stages of our response to the crisis in Moncton, our meetings were held in the NAV CANADA offices, even for the family members of employees, but soon after the crisis response team was in place, we decided to send them out to conduct home visits in Pinehurst, the locked-down area. By doing so, they were able to be with the families during the coping process. This led to discussions and storytelling with employees and their families over coffee and tea. It allowed our employees to focus on being not employees or spouses of employees, but moms and dads supporting their children and supporting one another. It also allowed children and teenagers to tell the story in their own way through stories and drawings that only a four-year-old or a teen could possibly share.

As is typically the case with effective leadership, NAV CANADA demonstrated its commitment to proceeding in collaboration with employees, as shown by how it handled an interesting development while responding to the event. The organization illustrated how taking a caring approach to supporting people can be a direct benefit to the relationship between the organization and the community.

When the crisis response team was in the community, something quite remarkable happened. When we were in the process of engaging the employees and their families in their homes, many of them began to express concern about their friends within the neighbourhood, people who had, like themselves, witnessed the shootings and lived through being locked down in their basements for almost a day and a half. Apparently conversations had taken place between the NAV CANADA employees and the other families in the community, and when the neighbours were told about the support that NAV CANADA was providing, they were interested, partly because they were not receiving similar services. Many of the NAV CANADA employees within the Pinehurst area came forward to the management group requesting that their neighbours and the families be given an opportunity to sit with our team in order to process the trauma. The management team did not hesitate, and issued a statement that if a friend, family member, or neighbour required support – in general meetings, one-on-ones, or even home visits – the service should be provided, at no cost and with no questions asked.

It wasn't really a decision on our part about whether we would offer the help. It was just the right thing to do. But it was also a way of ensuring that our employees, their families, and their communities knew that we were genuinely interested in their well-being.

Chapter Six

Stage One: Anticipating the Storm

Make your vision so powerful that when you finally accomplish your goal, you have a sense of déjà vu.

Cynthia Kersey

Key Concept: Build the Plan with Your People

When I work with a company to prepare for the possibility of a crisis, I take the company through a series of steps designed to develop a preparedness document that emphasizes employee wellness. Throughout this process, I advise organizational leaders to make their preparation decisions based on the core question of people-focused crisis leadership: what do the employees need?

I have seen many planning exercises that begin with human considerations wander off into long lists about resource allocation and alternate production scenarios. These issues are important matters for crisis management, but the piece that I add to any comprehensive plan has a different focus. I see how easily organizations turn their attention to financial, technological, or operational issues. Leaders who have never been in an actual crisis underestimate its effect on their people. From the safe confines of a pre-crisis planning session, it is difficult to imagine how things could get so bad that people are hardly able to function. I remember talking to an organizational leader of a multinational corporation after the 2011 tsunami hit Japan. He explained how he had followed the conventional wisdom: focus on the physical plant, systems, tasks, and resources to get back to regular productivity. He then said, "We got the offices running again, but we didn't prepare the people to come back to work. We didn't have a plan for the people. That was a mistake."

A good comprehensive plan includes a focus on people, because people drive the organization. But that is only part of the story. You also need to *involve* people in creating the plan. A brilliantly worded people-focused continuity plan written entirely by the senior management team without employee input is a dead document. Planning is as much about emotionally and mentally preparing people as it is about thinking through the issues you will face. People need time and conversation to integrate a new vision of the future, which helps make sure that your organization can respond when a storm comes. The quality of a plan also hinges on the involvement of employees, because they understand their part of the company better than you do. If you can engage your employees in fleshing out the details of how they will respond, you ensure that the planning will be as effective as possible.

Your end goal is to produce a written document that fits into your larger crisis management plan, accurately expresses the collective thinking, and leaves everyone feeling connected because it represents their ideas about how to approach an event. With the people-focused plan established, you can engage everyone in periodic reviewing, updating, and re-teaching of the plan – with the hope that you never have to put it into action.

When I work with companies to establish plans, I counsel them to use what I call a "wagon wheel review." This structure is designed to ensure maximal involvement and buy-in from employees because it requires input from all quarters. I use it in both the planning and reflection stages: the former for looking ahead, and the latter for looking back. In chapter eight, I outline the process of conducting a wagon wheel review in order to engage as many people as possible. Widespread engagement is critical. Every person, department, and division is different, and any successful crisis response will have layers of customized options that meet people where they are.

Saying that people come first and then painting them all with the same brush is not people-focused crisis leadership. The best possible planning never loses track of the need to allow for flexibility in application. Give everyone the basic resources they require for the response, but leave your plans open enough that managers and leaders can use their creativity and insight to take care of people. People-focused crisis leadership, by definition, is fluid.

To help leaders understand the balance between customization and protocol, I often use pharmacogenetics as a metaphor. Medical practitioners who customize a drug plan to the particular needs of a body are tailoring medication for the individual patient. Yes, there are some drug protocols that work for all people, but there are also many unique reactions within the biochemistry of a particular person. With this metaphor in mind, leaders grasp the idea of proceeding with options instead of rigid obligations, while having all necessary widespread resources and systems in place.

Most leaders know from experience that creativity is essential, even in large organizations where success requires structures and standard procedures. I remember when the Canadian Imperial Bank of Commerce (CIBC) hired me to work with its employees in the Cayman Islands. The leaders had to grapple with an extended power outage over the entire island. They had to set aside the "manual" and make decisions that made sense. There was nothing in the manual that predicted what they were dealing with. There could not have been. Their situation was living proof that good planning requires anticipating and setting the proper foundation in such a way that it is easy to use or set aside the plan as needed.

Prior to Hurricane Katrina hitting the Folgers plant in Slidell, Louisiana, Procter & Gamble already had extensive crisis plans in place as a result of its experiences with earthquakes in Kobe and Istanbul. Learning from experience put P&G in a position to properly prepare for future problems. As Tom Spedding explained:

We have a fairly significant disaster plan that we use when we have a sense that one of our facilities may be involved in an event, and we always encourage the leadership to look at it as a kind of check-list that they can use to get ready or respond. It's really important to have a plan in place so that you have the key resources in place if you need them. I think it also helps at P&G that I have been through this all before, so they know that I understand how to approach the crisis response properly, but the planning is critical to help set things up well. It really is true that when the leadership can set the goals and empower people to act, things are successful. Some companies talk about empowering their people but they don't. I think P&G is pretty good at it. It is a big company, so there can be frustrations at times, but when it comes to doing the right thing for our employees in a crisis, there is no second guessing what we do.

Even though P&G was very well prepared, and its communication systems were a part of that preparation, the hurricane caused a wrinkle that was entirely new for them: there was no way to reach out to people. They had to rely on call-ins. So they set up a call centre immediately – a kind of modified command centre. They were able to move quickly because P&G's crisis response plans already contained the framework needed for managing communication.

P&G is a model of planning and preparation. It has a history of involving employees in business continuity plans (BCPs), makes the necessary resource commitments required to prepare, and takes the training of its people seriously. In the particular case of Hurricane Katrina, the leadership worked continuously during the forty-eight hour period prior to the storm making landfall to minimize the damage to the Folgers operation.

The management did a great job anticipating the worst-case scenario when they knew the storm was coming. They anticipated that the plant would be flooded and that the employees would not be able to get back to it at all. So on the Saturday before the storm, they evacuated the plant and moved the majority of the raw materials, which are mainly coffee beans, to a location on higher ground that was well above sea level. They also tried to move the machinery in the plant to a separate location or to a higher place away from floor level as much as possible. This preparation was important because it meant that the recovery went more smoothly once we were able to get back in.

Having worked extensively with P&G, I know that their plans are highly people focused; most of the lessons that Tom spoke about, drawn from previous disaster management experiences, emphasized helping the employees cope with the fallout from the incident. Given its experience, P&G has been able to approach planning with the kind of attentiveness that direct crisis experience creates. The company was well prepared with the various supports that employees and families would need after Katrina, and even when the systems in place failed, it was well positioned to make changes quickly, such as engaging a new EAP provider on the fly.

Techniques for the Planning Stage

Break Your Planning into Three Phases

When advising businesses about creating their crisis response plans, I suggest three phases: imagine it, create it, and teach it.

Imagine it: Your planning should begin with the end in mind and help everyone envision and articulate the people-focused systems and procedures that will be required. This process involves challenging the committees from across the organization to make the impossible possible. Leaders often have to push people to consider all possible risks and responses, but the more imaginative they are, the more effective the plans will be. This is especially true when assessing the difference between essential services and peripheral functions. Planning for the "what ifs" is not just about imagining events that are hard to imagine. It is about knowing which of your business functions will determine your ability to weather a crisis.

Create it: Make sure the written plan contains every conceivable list, process description, policy guideline, and resource document that pertains to employee safety and wellness. Ensure that it includes evacuation plans and blueprints of the buildings, records of who works where, and plans for on-site medical care. Also ensure that there are pre-established "first response" teams drawn from your own staff for immediate needs such as cardiopulmonary resuscitation (CPR) or peer counselling. It is also a good idea to have a detailed outline of crisis leadership roles, especially since the way you allocate people may not reflect their normal roles.

Teach it: With the plans in place and written up, help your whole team engrain the habits required to execute the plans. This involves taking time and allocating funds to properly train everyone for whatever skills they will need. Not unlike an airline making sure that the cabin crew on a jet is trained to manage the emergency systems, you need to help your people develop habits. Students across the world suffer through evacuation drills for exactly the same reason: they need to respond to a fire without thinking. Crisis planning is no different. If you don't practice the potential situations your people will face, they will not be ready. Just talking about how to cope with an incident is not preparation.

Analyse Your Risks

Most businesses complete a vulnerability analysis chart by going through all aspects of the operation and assessing potential weaknesses. I emphasize that, when considering all internal and external risks – ways that you are exposed because of the nature of the business and the context in which it operates – you also need to consider ways in which your people are vulnerable owing to their role, geography, place in the organization, and so on. Create itemized inventories of all potential risks to your people and recommendations for how those risks can be mediated as best as possible. This analysis includes an assessment of your legal status in all areas, including insurance and benefits packages, since employees will require this support.

Imagine the worst-case scenario and talk through how it would affect your people. Look at the models around you, and be brutal about identifying your weaknesses. As an example, a camp or school that works with children has the possibility of a sexual abuse charge against one of its employees near the top of the list of potential risks. Acknowledging this risk allows the organization to prepare and plan accordingly with preventative measures and details about how it would respond to a crisis.

In particular, when assessing "exposures" related to people, think about your own version of what Thomas Homer-Dixon calls "keystone species." He uses an extended ecosystem metaphor to illustrate that certain species function to sustain the entire system.[1] Particular plants whose pollen ensures the effective reproduction of their species are essential to life up and down the food chain, and any significant damage to a keystone species can have a devastating effect. Sort out who among your people are "keystone species" so you can see where your risk level is particularly high. Which people, if unable to function, would leave your business crippled? What have you done to protect the organization against this risk? In a crisis, considering the role that particular people play in the overall system is very important.

When Bonnie Adamson arrived in her role as CEO of North York General Hospital, she was faced with several major organizational needs that had to be addressed right away because they had a limiting effect on her ability to establish proper risk management protocols.

When I came in, I was replacing a long-tenured CEO who was well respected and had built up a positive image for the hospital in the community and great pride inside the organization. But during an external review in the spring of 2002 prior to me arriving in the job, it was revealed that there were some serious culture issues to be addressed that had been left unattended for some time. It was an organization that was not used to a lot of change, and the history had been that the Ontario Ministry of Health and Long-Term Care just provided more money each year, which meant there had been very little incentive to address existing issues.

What Bonnie experienced was a harsh reality of an organization's ability to properly prepare for any potential crisis: if there are not sufficient and efficiently allocated resources to support people, it is difficult to respond to emergencies. In large organizations, there are complex issues, but a strong leader will wade into the fray with an emphasis on establishing preparedness in all areas.

When I arrived in August, I was greeted with the following crisis: the money expected from the Ministry did not materialize, which meant the hospital's deficit was quite large and a change was required. There was also a large capital expansion underway, so there was construction everywhere. The organization was unable to meet payroll, and there were no business recovery plans in place. By the end of first week, the senior team and I, with support from the Ministry of Health, undertook our own operational review to find efficiencies. This caused some uneasiness in the organization, but it was a critical step for us to take. Over the fall, as the new CEO and by involving all of the staff in a review process, we set out a new vision for the hospital and made some changes at the senior level. These moves caused a bit more unrest, but by Christmas time many of the changes were in place with plans for more to come in order to balance the fiscal situation. The Ministry was supporting NYGH to ensure we could meet payroll and supported our plan to restabilize financially, which we were well on our road to doing when SARS hit.

When the SARS crisis began, and many of the key issues she had identified still needed to be addressed, Bonnie and her team moved risk management to the top of their list of concerns as part of their on-the-fly preparation for the crisis once it had already hit.

I realized right away that our risk management processes required drastic improvement immediately to address the dramatic change in our environment. They had been designed for the "old" world. One of the first things I did was to appoint a vice-president special projects – SARS risk management and quality. The mandate was to create the best possible program to address our situation with renewed structures and processes as soon as possible, using external assistance as needed. It was restructuring in real time based on the urgent organizational need. There was a constant reassessment of the priority needs of the organization. I remember saying that the whole experience was like working in an intensive care unit where each patient arrests one at a time repeatedly. It was like a war zone.

Audit the Skills of Your People

You never know what you have until you know what you have. Organizations tend not to make a full inventory of their people's skills. Waiting until you need different skills than are normally required is not the best approach. Be aware of what your people can do in advance by performing a skills audit. Give people a chance to tell you about all the amazing things they can do – no matter how irrelevant they seem to the nature of your business. The employee who is a plumber on the side may be of use in the moment if water starts flooding in. The amateur poet could come in handy if demands for communication skyrocket, and you are short on word-smiths. The staffer who is a certified CPR instructor could literally save lives. The accounts payable clerk who speaks five languages because she grew up in the heart of Eastern Europe could be a huge help if people from various cultures are trying to work together.

Work on the assumption that all skills are worth assessing, and take the time to ask people what they can do. Not only does this give you the information you might need, but asking your employees about their interests and background also gives them a sense that you value them beyond their current role. The skills audit will also help you see interests that may be directly relevant to an individual employee's career path, along with talents you might draw on if you get into the kind of reassignment that inevitably occurs in a crisis as absenteeism rises and the demands of the situation change. All told, there is no downside to learning about your employees' hidden talents, especially when this information can be collected in non-threatening and fun ways that benefit everyone.

Beyond the random skills people have, you will want to focus on leadership potential in particular. List your people based on their take-charge qualities by using metrics that assess leadership ability – especially when direct leadership is not a central part of a person's daily work. Annual reviews tend to focus on the skills required for a person's current role. If you make a "leadership skills inventory" part of an annual review or another form of self, peer, or supervisor assessment, you will gather the information that you need. You will also inspire people to think of themselves as leaders. Employees keep a close eye on what the organization measures. Asking about leadership potential emphasizes qualities that will improve your operations long before a storm comes – a wonderful side effect of careful crisis planning. Of course, also make sure you are proactive about assessing and supporting leadership development in your managers, because leadership qualities are far more present in people than you might think. Most people just need help bringing them to the surface.

Lyne Wilson explained to me that in 1989, prior to the organization becoming NAV CANADA, Anne Logie, a nurse working for what was then Transport Canada, recognized that air traffic controllers (ATCs) who had been exposed to tragic accidents and near misses were experiencing the symptoms of what we would now call post-traumatic stress disorder. She and an ATC named Mike Dooling convinced the Canadian Air Traffic Control Association to cover the costs for critical incident response training, and together they went to the United States to be certified by the Critical Incident Stress Foundation.

On 19 July 1989, United Airlines Flight 232 was scheduled to fly from Stapleton International Airport in Denver, Colorado, to O'Hare International Airport in Chicago. The DC-10, carrying 296 people, crashed at the Sioux Gateway Airport in Sioux City, Iowa, as a result of a system failure of its tail-mounted engine. Shrapnel within the engine was hurled at a very high speed into the hydraulic lines and penetrated all three independent hydraulic systems on board the aircraft. Altogether, 111 people died as a result of the accident, and another 185 survived, many suffering various forms of physical and psychological injury.[2]

Lyne Wilson explained the fortuitous timing of the training:

> The crash took place shortly after Anne and Mike had returned from their training. The organization reached out to them to provide assistance to the air navigation staff involved in the event. Because they were staff members who had acquired specialized crisis response skills, they had credibility with people and were able to help while also beginning the process of developing a critical incident peer team. Initially, the peer team was a union-run program, but within a few years, Transport Canada recognized the intrinsic value of this kind of support structure, and it became a joint investment supported by both management and the union.

In many ways, the United Airlines Flight 232 crash served as the catalyst in the air traffic control profession to build, train, and sustain CISM support teams in an effort to better ensure that those in the field maintain a healthy psychological state.

Prior to the Moncton RCMP shootings in the summer of 2014, NAV CANADA had established a critical incident response team consisting of approximately 150 members spread out all across Canada and representing the various roles in their client services continuum. As Lyne explained, "By June 4th, we had not only expanded the peer team's service spectrum to include flight service specialists and air traffic operations specialists, but we had also trained members from each of these disciplines to become contributing participants on their peer support team."

In 2012, when NAV CANADA contracted me to conduct comprehensive large-scale events/disaster response training, it had already taken its entire national critical incident peer support team to another level. This advance afforded the same members who had been providing support to their colleagues after experiencing job-related tragic events to be trained in how to assess and respond to catastrophic occurrences such as large-scale plane crashes, natural disasters, and terrorist activities.

Our goal in working with the NAV CANADA staff was not to turn the team into lay therapists, but to arm them with the necessary insights to engage people in real conversation when they came forward with an issue by asking good questions, gathering information, and facilitating an appropriate referral. That goal was achieved, and the combination of their basic defusing skills and newly acquired large-scale events response repertoire meant that the NAV CANADA team was well positioned to move into Moncton, New Brunswick, to provide the support that the staff and their family members required.

"NAV CANADA is committed to assessing and promoting the development of skills for our people," said Lyne. "We work hard to make sure we have a strong level of preparedness for disaster response. The initiative that started as a new skillset for a few employees has become a program for the entire organization."

Take Care of Employees and Their Families

In keeping with my emphasis on the whole person, I advise businesses to be explicit about the supports that will be in place for employees and their families. I encourage leaders to develop "emotional re-entry" plans to outline the phases of a return-to-work approach. I use the analogy that emotional re-entry is like the diver who needs to come to the surface slowly to adjust to the pressure at each level. Emotional adjustment takes time and varies from person to person. By including plans to accommodate employees with staggered work hours, providing EAP options such as group support sessions or individual counselling, and creating lists of supplies that might be needed, the company can go a long way towards preparing for the worst. It is also critical that an organization's attention extend to direct supports for family members. Employees are only as effective in their work as their overall context allows, and the enormous stress of family issues is a hindrance when trying to get back to work. Ultimately, planning to actively support people and their families means taking action on an empathic impulse as opposed to paying lip service to the idea that people matter.

Plan Your Communications Command Centre

I mentioned the need for a communications command centre in the chapter on communication, but I would be remiss if I did not emphasize it here. If you do not plan out the logistical and operational aspects of a crisis communication system, you will be incapable of managing information demands, and you will lose the most important connection you have with your people. A communications command centre needs to be located in a central place that can be easily accessed by as many employees as possible in order to have technological and practical resources to manage the flow of information. You should also prearrange all aspects of your systems: communication trees, updated personnel information, spaces where you can hold large-scale meetings with staff, contingency plans for alternate modes of interaction, and detailed outlines of responsibilities for management, including specific roles such as "primary spokesperson" or "employee family liaison." Also include a detailed plan for media relations and job descriptions of all members of the communications team.

One of the central issues faced by Nancy Tower and the leadership team at Nova Scotia Power during the response to Hurricane Juan was communication with the public. In the face of huge power outages, and in an era before social media, widespread cellular use, and satellite communication, they had to be very creative. They followed their plan and were proactive about getting into the media to give the public fair warning about what was coming.

> Prior to Juan, we had been in contact with the media. The media is a big part of our preparation. We were in the media warning people that the hurricane was coming. It was interesting that Nova Scotians didn't think it was going to be that bad; there are media clips of people saying, "What hurricane"? That was Sunday during the day, and the hurricane hit Sunday at midnight. Because people didn't really think it was going to be that bad, they really didn't have a sense of what they needed to do to prepare. Things like filling your bathtub with water

or getting cash out of the machine or filling up your car with gas. Or getting dried goods because your fridge and freezer may not work.

Extend Your Planning for Business Not As Usual

When laying out your crisis preparations, think about how you would manage if your operations were radically interrupted. Begin by establishing an "incident fund" that allocates money on an annual basis to disaster protection. If you arrive at fiscal year-end and the money has not been needed to cope with an incident, you can reallocate the funds. But having the money set aside is a significant step towards protecting the company against an irrecoverable shock. Also, create a virtual office plan (VOP) to sort through how you will run your operations if the main offices are destroyed or incapacitated in some way. This plan includes practices that some firms, especially information-based operations like IT companies and financial institutions, use for alternative sites and networks. You will also need to map out staffing provisions if large numbers of your people are offline for a significant amount of time. An incident will require a high degree of creativity in human resource allocation, but if you have a model to work from you will be off to a good start; creating options from scratch in the middle of the storm is not a good idea.

Nova Scotia Power is a great example of this kind of preparation. Prior to Juan, it established mutual assistance agreements with surrounding jurisdictions' power companies. Should any of the power utilities experience challenges that limited their people's ability to respond to the event, as is commonly the case after a tropical storm, other utilities would be willing to step forward and assist each other where required.

LEADERSHIP SUMMARY

Key Concept
- *Build your people-focused crisis response plan with your people*: create a specialized section of your comprehensive business continuity

plan tailored to the needs and ideas of all departments that emphasizes flexibility and creativity for managers to respond to the uncertain conditions of a crisis.

Techniques
- *Break your planning into three stages – imagine, create, and teach*: help your entire team envision various worst-case scenarios, create a ready-to-use response plan, and take time to engrain various crisis response habits.
- *Analyse your risks*: understand the organizational vulnerabilities related to personnel that, if disrupted, will cripple the business.
- *Audit the skills of your people*: assess the job-related, industry-related, leadership, and personal capacities of your employees in order to have a clear picture of what people can contribute in the event of a crisis.
- *Take care of your employees and their families*: think of the needs of employees' families as identical to their own.
- *Plan the communication command centre*: ensure that the tangible, practical needs of a command centre – such as technology, lists, processes, and personnel assignments – are clearly outlined and known.
- *Extend your planning for business not as usual*: budget and plan as if there will be a crisis every year so that you are always ready to respond.

Chapter Seven

Stage Two: In the Eye of the Storm

The only safe ship in a storm is leadership.

Faye Wattleton

Key Concept: Be Prepared to Make Tough Decisions

Immediately following an incident, your task is to assess the damage. Even before you initiate the company's well-crafted BCP, you have to know what you are dealing with. An extensive impact assessment will collect as much data from as many sources as possible. This assessment can coincide with setting up the command centre, but you should not wait to have organized and centralized communication in place. It is normal and natural for communication in the early stages of a crisis to be fragmented and intermittent. Focus on getting the available information and establishing what has happened. Remember: the more you can be a person first and a manager second, the better. Employees will mostly be off balance and confused in the early stages, and you should not feel that you have to be highly "leaderly" at this point. I advocate open and informal interactions between leaders and workers at all times, but this type of interaction is especially critical in the moments following an event. Collect key people around you – some of whom may not be the management team – and work together honestly and rapidly to take an inventory of losses and risks. Look at all aspects of the business: the production and customer base, the state of the organization's culture, the status of equipment and resources, and the effect on employees and their families. The more detailed your inventory, the more you can accurately direct resources. Just remember to protect against the inevitable pressure to make practical, logistical, and material considerations your primary focus. People-focused crisis leadership means putting your employees first. If the inventory of losses you create allows object considerations to dominate your thinking, you are off to a bad start.

Once you have a sense of what you are dealing with, launch the BCP with a focus on people first. If you have done your homework, everyone in the company will know what to do and how to do it. Use the plan as a basic framework, and begin with the most pressing needs. Similar to a power company trying to get the lights back on after a hurricane, you will likely begin at the base of Maslow's hierarchy – with issues like food and shelter – and then work towards complex and personal issues such as the effects of dislocation and loss. Resist pressure to meet needs that are secondary. Everyone will think that their area or concern is paramount. You need to delineate and allocate resources accordingly. Whenever possible, explain why you have proceeded as you have, but do not let every problem seem huge. Prioritize or you will be swamped by the wave of issues you have to address.

Establishing priorities will force you to make hard calls: some decisions will be unpopular with your employees, their families, your administrative team, and the community. These decisions require mental toughness, a capacity to suffer scrutiny, and an ability to handle personal attacks. These leadership moments are defining, and you have to stand in the spotlight and say, "I am responsible for that." More than anything, people need to see you lead. Even if they don't agree with the direction you are taking, they will respond to the strength of character required to be accountable. I remember Larry Morden, vice-president of human resources at North York General Hospital, shutting down 256 union grievances regarding SARS when he concluded that they would not benefit anyone – including the people looking for compensation – and Jim MacLean shutting down the ER at Markham Stouffville Hospital, and Howard Lutnick at Cantor Fitzgerald adjusting salaries for employees so that he could set aside 25 per cent of the profit for the next five years to give to victims' families. These leaders took a great deal of heat, but their strength shone through, and they won loyalty and support as a result.

The complexity of the initial responses to a crisis and the tough decisions that follow are so significant that I want to offer an example from each of the four profiled leaders.

Nova Scotia Power – Nancy Tower

In describing the process that NSP went through to learn and build its protocols following the storm, Nancy Tower articulated several critical elements of the nature of crisis response in the moment. Her focus emphasizes not only the intense pressure of time and impact that a leader faces, but some of the central considerations that have to be in play for those decisions.

> Afterward, when we were reviewing what happened and updating our protocols, there was some conversation about storm coordination needing to be collaborative. But I pointed out that it might seem like that is the best option, but when a storm comes, there is no time to get a vote and have discussion. It has to be set up so that the storm lead gathers information and then makes a decision. Although there is collective involvement, there must be no confusion about how the decisions get made. You need to be able to make the decisions in the moment. One of the lessons I learned in this is that collaboration has its place, but decisions have to be made that take courage.
>
> Sometimes to get the staff required, crews have to travel a distance. But if you want to make the deadline for the restoration, then you have to make a decision and get those crews on the road. You don't have a lot of time. Someone said to me during one of the drills we did afterward, "I would likely have called my boss to talk to him about the decisions."

I explained that I would not have had time. I needed to know before the event how he thinks about certain things. I needed to have broad parameters in place, and the restoration plans would have to include them. You have to be able to make decisions in the moment and believe that even if he doesn't agree with the exact decision, he has enough confidence in me to know that I made the best decision given the information that I have at my disposal. It's about having confidence. That way, if you make a decision and the collective wisdom looking back is that you made a mistake, at least people know that you had the experience and skill you needed, and that you made what you thought was the best decision under the circumstances. When you are making the decision, you can't be second guessing yourself. But it is also so important not to act in isolation. If you have a team around you, listen to what they are saying. Be a good listener, and hear what they are saying and what they are not saying. And ask good questions.

NAV CANADA – Lyne Wilson

NAV CANADA's response to the shootings in Moncton illustrates both its fluid response to the resource needs of the crisis response team and its understanding of the importance of providing assistance tailored to the needs of people.

> When the crisis response teams were arriving in Moncton, we were executing the Level 2 Large-Scale Events Training we had participated in so that the computers, phones, chargers, and general office supplies required to establish the on-location command centre were available and ready for the command centre manager and NAV CANADA nurse, Trish Bell, to hit the ground running once her plane touched down.

When setting up the crisis response team, Lyne Wilson was clear about the need to have a team that could meet geographic, linguistic, and cultural needs so that the helpers and the helped could relate to one another. This process included asking important questions: Are people English speaking, French speaking, and/or is there another primary language spoken by the employees and their family members? Is the group composed of air traffic controllers, flight services specialists, air traffic operations specialists, technologists, engineers, administrative staff, or a combination of all of these? Is there a large management or senior management contingent? Is the event happening in a northern or remote community where the employees have been imported to service the area and are away from their families? What are some of the life stages of the employees whom we are about to serve? Do they have young families, children in school, spouses in careers, or are they a more senior group whose families and relationships are long established? Are the employees and family members in the identified location known to one another – are they friends, do they have a history in the community, or are they transients, there to complete a work term and then exit?

All these factors have to be part of a leader's calculation when considering an assistance team in order for "helpers to be of help." NAV CANADA has done this very well throughout its history, but according to Lyne the Moncton tragedy and the team's subsequent response cemented this practice moving forward.

Once the team was selected and underway, the first order of business was to bring them all together for an update on what was happening in the Pinehurst community. The update included how many staff and families had been locked down, their current status, and the status of all other Moncton Centre NAV CANADA personnel outside the Pinehurst area.

In keeping with the training, the team went through a forecasting exercise wherein they speculated, in an educated fashion, about what our staff in Pinehurst had experienced, their physical, emotional, and familial responses, and their current and future needs. With these notions in mind, the team was able to match the staff's needs with the services that we as group could provide.

That same evening, the crisis team and I met with the management team for the Moncton NAV CANADA location. Our goal was to introduce the two parties – our crisis response team of peers and clinicians to the managers – and to access the management team's insights about what had happened, the current conditions, the personnel that caused them some worry, areas of vulnerability among the staff, and the influence the event has or could have on the air traffic operations. This was a "needs assessment meets service provision plan" kind of meeting. The last thing we did, which may well have been the most important of our contributions that evening, was to discuss with the management team their own personal experiences and those of their families throughout this whole affair.

Procter & Gamble – Tom Spedding

Tom Spedding outlined how the situation in Slidell led to the extended difficulties that come with extensive damage and destruction following a major event like a hurricane. P&G's response to the difficulties is an example of creative modification to normal approaches, putting the needs of employees first, and ensuring that there is access to adequate funding for resources.

> The biggest frustration we've always had with these kinds of natural disasters is, How do you account for the people? When you can't find everyone, you are always trying to come up with better ways to be able to get in touch with your employees or have them get in touch with you so that you know what their status is. With Katrina, it was the first time we encountered a situation where there was absolutely no way to outreach to them because the phones, Internet, mail, and all forms of communication were stopped, at least for some period of time. We had to rely on our employees to call us. We set up a call centre with a 1-800 number in nearby Alexandria where we happened to have another plant. The HR manager from New Orleans went to Alexandria on the Saturday before the storm and set up an "on-call" team. Some people called us on cell phones, but the satellites were overloaded, so they often got a busy signal. We had to rely on word of mouth to let people know that they should call in and inform us

about their status. It took us about two weeks before we were sure that we had heard from every employee, but we were eventually able to determine that all five hundred of our people who worked and lived in the area were alive. There were no fatalities, so we were very fortunate, but everyone was touched by the devastation. Their homes were flooded, or maybe their parents' home or an aunt's or uncle's. Everybody suffered from the storm, primarily from water damage due to flooding. When they were first getting in touch with us, the incentive for them to call was that they wanted to know three things: Do I still have a job? When will the plant restart? Is there anything the company can do to help get me some cash?

North York General Hospital – Bonnie Adamson

On the day that SARS hit the hospital, Bonnie Adamson had been away in the morning at a meeting. Her description of her return outlines how an effective leader copes with what is happening as it happens by prioritizing and getting the team focused.

When I arrived back at the hospital and entered the command centre, I could quickly see the challenges facing our committed and highly stressed team. The Ministry of Health and Long-Term Care was sending multiple directives, emails, and faxes on a frequent basis and scheduling many teleconferences, continuously assessing the status across the Toronto hospitals. At NYGH, multiple patients had been admitted with SARS, the operating rooms were working overtime, and the emergency department was exceedingly busy and on high alert.

As I was integrating into the command centre team, I listened to multiple pieces of patient and related information from multiple sources being communicated in various ways. I realized quickly that what we needed was a systematic way to look at the whole organization with all the moving parts. I went back to my early years of nursing supervision when we had to look at the whole organization each shift to see the overall activity and where areas of crisis or difficulty are with patients or staffing. We asked questions like, What's the total census? How many staff do you have? Where are the greatest areas of need? Where do you redistribute the staff? Where are the sickest or most unstable patients? I slipped immediately into that mode asking, "What is the big picture here?" I translated my previous experience into some communication and planning structures to facilitate key organization-wide questions. This new framework allowed the command centre team to systematically assess and plan hour by hour and day by day the set of circumstances we were experiencing in this uncharted clinical territory. As we went along, we found that daily or more frequent communication was necessary in order to keep all five thousand people at NYGH informed of the changing situation.

The SARS crisis was so widespread that many levels of leadership were involved in managing the situation, which put Bonnie in a position of having to make decisions about how to proceed in the face of sometimes conflicting direction and needs. One particular example was the process she and her team went through of moving a high-profile program out of the hospital.

I was dealing with the Ministry of Health senior officials, including the deputy minister calling regarding many of our decisions. For example, the decision to move obstetrics out of NYGH and distribute those patients across other hospitals required significant discussion. Our rationale was that we could not guarantee the safety of these patients from contracting the SARS virus. Because of my clinical background, I understood very clearly the concerns of the staff and physician leaders. After careful consideration from all perspectives, I approved the recommended decision made jointly by physician and hospital leaders to triage the obstetrical patients to eight other hospitals in the region. Obstetrics was a star program, and there was some resistance to the move. By transferring the patients out of our hospital, we were creating a greater sense of loss for our people and at the same time putting a burden on eight other hospitals. The prospect of losing the positive community reputation for this service and the potential that mothers

may never return to NYGH to have a baby in the future created significant anticipatory stress. However, patient safety was the imperative. Needless to say, the senior Ministry staff were very concerned
and asked many, many questions to clearly understand our position.
It was all about patient safety. The day after the decision, a medical
resident from NYGH was diagnosed with SARS. We were very happy
that we had made this very tough decision. This was a gut judgment
rather than a decision based on evidence or textbook information. The
decision was made as a senior team. We could not take a chance that
mothers and babies could be at risk of contracting the deadly virus. To
continue to deliver babies in this situation would have been irrespon-
sible. It was a social accountability. Thankfully, no one associated with
that program became ill.

Our staff were totally committed to protecting the safety of our
obstetrical patients and rose above any negativity. The staff kept in
contact with the patients via telephone throughout their hospitaliza-
tion in other settings and focused on making the temporary situation
work for the patients, for other hospitals, and for NYGH staff and physicians. The nurses and physicians never lost the patient–family connection. The patients were very impressed, and after the unit opened
again, the volumes became higher than prior to SARS. Any time we
see a pregnant woman in the elevator or in the halls, it is a source of
pride for all of us that these patients were so well cared for by our
teams during the difficult period.

Bonnie also dealt with huge staffing issues and had to be firm and
creative in finding ways to ensure that the hospital was properly
staffed. The intensity of the work required by the crisis also meant
Bonnie had to cope with compensation issues for staff, a complex
process at the best of times, which became very challenging during
the crisis's demands for high-speed problem solving.

There was a shortage of intensive care nurses. I called London and
Ottawa to see if any intensive care nurses would assist us. My attempts
were unsuccessful. We were relying on agency nurses from an external

company to augment our staff numbers. One night, there were complaints regarding competencies of some agency nurses who, due to company contracts with the hospital, were receiving higher pay than our staff. A system was designed to ensure consistency in quality and preparedness of agency nurses to care for these critically ill patients. The quality of care concerns led us to finalize a decision to go to the Board to request approval to pay wages higher than the contractual agreement. Our preference was to have NYGH staff care for these patients.

We wanted to compensate our staff properly for the reality of the situation by setting up a system for staff to receive double pay if working in the SARS units. This was very difficult because these actions would go against the union contracts. There was no provision in the union contract for such a consideration. For several days, we relentlessly attempted to convince the Ministry and the Ontario Hospital Association that this was the right decision. The provincial concern was that this decision could have negative long-term system impact with contract bargaining. However, at NYGH, our staff were literally working in life-threatening environments, a situation that never had existed in our memory. Staff started to refuse to come to work unless we provided increased pay. Some of their colleagues were contracting this disease and were hospitalized at NYGH. Despite lack of support externally, as the CEO, I presented to the Board the context of the problem and our recommended decision. The NYGH Board of Directors approved our plan, and the double time system was initiated. This action demonstrated to our staff that we understood the risk they were facing and that we respected and valued them.

The union contract issue was a major barrier to supporting our staff. Staff were nervous and very fearful about their health and the health of their families because they worked at NYGH. I remember the anger of the intensive care staff. They were fighting the disease on the frontline and were incredibly frustrated with what they perceived to be a lack of support from the leadership and a lack of understanding as to how hard the work was for them. They wanted increased pay for working in this environment. As an administrative team, we had been doing as much as possible to get the system parties to cooperate with us on the pay issue and help them to understand the realities of the staff. Increased payment was viewed by staff as a sign of recognition and was extremely important to them. There was no sense telling the staff about our challenges because it would not have been meaningful to them and would have likely increased their frustration. It would simply have made the situation worse by likely insulting them by talking about contract difficulties when they were immersed in a life-and-death situation. You have to go to where they are at. They do not need to worry about your issues. It was critically important to go outside the contract despite opposition in order for our excellent, committed, and exhausted staff to know that we supported them and that there was fairness regarding compensation.

Ultimately, others came to see that the collective bargaining agreement does not apply in a situation like SARS. In future contracts, language will be negotiated to address such a crisis scenario. As time has gone on, people now see that our decision did not destroy collective bargaining. Our priority was achieving a positive and safe outcome for our patients and staff.

Techniques during the Crisis

Allocate Your People by Talent, Not Job Description

In *The Upside of Down,* Thomas Homer-Dixon writes about systems that exhibit emergent properties: the whole is greater than the sum of the components.[1] When advising leaders, I use this idea to highlight that people's skills and qualities, when put together in new and interesting ways, may yield unforeseen creativity that can expedite the response process. Businesses are familiar with cross-pollination in the context of mergers, interdepartmental work groups, and think tanks, but leaders often try to solve problems using people above a certain floor or at a particular compensation level.

In a crisis, leaders need to embrace the counterintuitive thinking that new clusters of talent can create solutions that were not evident.

As an example, I have seen dozens of situations where the command centre is operated by people from throughout the organization who are not defined by their salary level. They just help. Non-homogenous teams generate creativity because members bring different perspectives and approaches, triggering a productive tension between ideas, which leads to new and innovative solutions and eliminates the fixed thought patterns of pre-established work groups. If the senior managers make it happen, the company can experience its own version of vacuum induction theory: leaders will emerge to fill a void. More than at any other time, a crisis needs to be an "egoless" environment, because there is no time for people to fuss about getting credit or looking good. Whoever is best suited to complete a task needs to do it. If you make skills and qualities the emphasis for assigning roles – not job descriptions – you let the right people lead.

Some people have what I call a higher thought unit per minute (TU/M) rate than others, and a leader's job is to find out who these people are. A high TU/M rate means that under pressure a person can take in, understand, and express ideas and information at a rapid rate. Some jobs require increased processing speed – such as EMS workers, air traffic controllers, and military leadership – but there are often employees at any level of an organization who process events and issues more quickly than their current role requires. If you are ready to enlist their help when the storm comes because you have already measured their capacity, you will be better prepared. You can also increase the TU/M rate simply by creating highly functional non-homogenous groups, because creativity and divergent thinking lead to speed. (A side effect of an emphasis on TU/M ability can be a kind of post-crisis headache if a person who was a central player in the response goes back to a less central role in the organization, but those issues can get resolved by finding ways for people's newly discovered talents to be applied.)

Processing speed is connected to ingenuity. Homer-Dixon is well known for his description of the "ingenuity gap" he believes technology has created: an increasing amount of information met with an increasingly limited ability to cope with it.[2] In my experience, a crisis narrows organization-specific ingenuity gaps, so a focus on structures that leverage this quality is beneficial. Some people are simply more creative under pressure – especially in life-and-death situations – because the mental and physical energy allocated to solving problems is radically increased as organizations allocate resources on a full-time basis, creating fewer mental limitations and a steady stream of inventive solutions. If you add ingenuity to the skills you audit, you will pre-screen for this quality and have a sense of where the organization's creativity lies.

Non-homogenous teams also take advantage of people's instincts. In a crisis, people's true colours come to the surface as they rely on innate reactions and inclinations that lie beneath any of the leadership, communication, or relationship courses they have taken. No amount of training and preparation can change what a person is under the surface. The catch is that when ingrained tendencies arise, they may or may not be helpful. Some people step it up and others cower. Keep in mind that no matter what you have done to prepare for an incident, you won't really be sure who you can count on until you are in a situation. Some people are just made for calm and level-headed leadership under pressure. If you approach the complex task of people allocation with a general disregard for official position, you will be able to assess raw instincts as you go and optimize the quality of the organization's response.

As she led the hospital through the SARS crisis, Bonnie Adamson had to constantly assess the efforts of employees at all levels of the organization, especially the leadership, in an effort to align the skills of her people with the needs of the situation.

The occupational health and safety program required additional strength in order to meet the growing and pressing needs of staff. The demands of our staff were far greater than the resources in this important program. The pressure on the leaders of NYGH was relentless. All leaders, hospital and physician, were working very long hours seven days a week in a very stressful situation. Many leaders handled the stress impressively well. They were highly energized and were amazing at meeting the needs of staff, patients, and families in extraordinary ways. As well, emerging leaders were becoming apparent at every level of the organization. On the other hand, other experienced leaders surprisingly did not handle the stress well and required significant support. Some responded to the highly charged situation with authoritarian behaviour, which caused unnecessary stress on others in an already emotionally charged environment. Observing the total leadership team at all levels in this crisis identified two existing leadership styles: authoritarian and stewardship/collaborative. At times, tension was evident between the two as they worked together.

Faced with this sudden crisis, we went into crisis management of the first order and just kept shifting priorities and assigning the best leaders and teams to each issue to be resolved. We had exceptionally strong medical leadership. In fact, the strength of our medical leadership as part of the command centre team assisted greatly in resolving a large number of difficult issues quickly and confidently. There was a true sense of community between the hospital and medical leaders. A strong bond was formed that has been sustained over time.

Deal with Simple Problems to Solve Complex Issues

The complexity of issues that arise in a storm is a huge challenge. When a situation seems too large, too multifaceted, and too intricate, we feel as if there is no way we can ever tackle it. But, as the saying goes, a ten-thousand-mile journey begins with a single step. You just have to start.

I advise corporate leaders to think of a complex situation as a collection of simple problems. Usually, you can begin by addressing the most basic needs and then break all the large issues into smaller chunks. Follow the lead of your people. Employees will be able to give you a sense of what is happening in various areas, and that information, collected through your command centre, will help you triage issues and decrease the sensation of helplessness and confusion. In disaster response, this approach to simple problems often means that the leaders need to get out and help with the sandbags or bucket brigade. This kind of activity connects you to people right away, and it also puts you at the frontlines so you are aware of people's basic needs. Just like a person rehabilitating from a major injury, make small, concerted efforts to rebuild the strength of the organization instead of rushing back to activity without proper healing. You have to cover the basics first.

Procter & Gamble's approach to helping its employees get back on their feet after Katrina began with a focus on very simple needs. The company worked its way through one need at a time to create a comprehensive response. As Tom Spedding explained:

A lot of people lost their credit cards, and whatever money they had with them was all they had. So one of the first things we did was to arrange for every employee to get a $5000 no-interest loan. We made money available to people right from the get go with no questions asked. It was a loan with very lax terms about when they would have to pay it back. We also learned very quickly that people were not able to return to their homes because they were under water or damaged to the point where they were uninhabitable, so we knew that we were going to have to do something about housing. We started right away trying to buy all the travel trailers we could, like a lot of other people were doing, and FEMA [Federal Emergency Management Agency], the federal government, came in and ended up helping with that. We ended up getting around one hundred or so fairly large trailers, and we literally set up a city in the parking lot of the plant that was flooded, once we were able to get in, and made the trailers available to people so that they would have a place to stay right away and after the plant was up and running.

Another part of the early response process was that we knew we needed to provide primary healthcare right away because the hospitals were shut down and most doctors' practices were not operating. We set up a clinic in one of the trailers staffed by nurses from Cincinnati who would go down there for a week and then come back up here. One problem with the nurses was that they did not have a license to practice in Louisiana, so they could only function as a medical technician at first, taking blood pressures and doing basic care. Then the Governor of Louisiana stepped in and arranged for a waiver that gave them temporary privileges and meant they were cleared to practice as a registered nurse until a certain date. At that point, they were able to start doing counselling and treating injuries and giving immunizations. It was a big deal, because we had not considered that and they were of limited value when they could not practice.

We also started to bring in food, a sort of meals on wheels. Our cafeteria vendors responded by providing mobile units for food, and they were providing hot meals as soon as they were able to set up in the trailer village. It was a full course meal, and the nurses were there to monitor the food to try to eliminate any problems with gastrointestinal upsets and make sure the food was edible.

Be Open to Learning and New Ways of Thinking

In his 1998 book *The Learning Paradox*, leadership consultant Jim Harris speaks of the paradoxical position most corporations and employees find themselves in: the very things that they fear the most – learning, changing, and coping with uncertainty – are the things most needed to succeed in business today.[3] He goes on to suggest that a person must move through the steps of learning, unlearning, and relearning again and again to ensure growth and avoid failure.

When an incident occurs, it creates change at every level of an organization. What was yesterday is no longer today. Once the crisis strikes, it is leaders' ability to unlearn what they have previously learned that leads to success in the face of the crisis. To hold steadfast to the tried and true ways of managing an organization is a road map for failure.

Tom Spedding of Procter & Gamble is an example of a leader who applied his learning as he moved from one catastrophic event to another. But what made him stand out was his clarity that each subsequent crisis would be different from the last and would include novel challenges.

Keep Track of People's Emotional Means

As I said earlier, I push leaders to think about their employees as a valuable asset, and I find that financial analogies can also be useful when sorting out how to work "within your means." People are accustomed to conceiving of spending decisions based on available money, so I ask them to modify their thinking to include "emotional means" in their calculations about what is possible. Monitoring and tracking emotional resources is hard, but you have to know how resilient your people are or you can end up in a mess. Leaders who pay heed to this idea are less likely to put unrealistic expectations into the system, because they engage in slow but long-lasting recovery to ensure success for the company and the workers. These leaders also look for ways to increase employees' emotional means through counselling and support services for them and their families.

Even though Procter & Gamble is a large organization, Tom Spedding and his team were very careful about tracking the state of their people – including the ones providing support to the displaced employees. As he explained:

> About a week after the flooding, I was in touch with the HR manager at Alexandria, which is two hours north of New Orleans, and she was telling me that the call team was working extensive hours and hearing all of the trauma and the carnage and the sad stories that happened to people. She was concerned about the overall health and well-being of the call centre, so not only did we have to be sorting out how to help our employees, we also had to provide support for the call centre people who were taking the calls. In fact, because we were able to get to them right away, the call centre workers and the people on the response team were the first ones that we provided counselling support for because we could. Then we could start to think about how to do our critical incident debriefings with the employees. When we did get to providing psychological support, our existing EAP wasn't available, so we contacted another operation, and they agreed to start providing support. We have subsequently given them our contract.

Watch for Repeated Traumas

The phrase "cumulative stress" can be misunderstood in the realm of crisis response. People often use the term to refer to the multiple demands on our time and energy that create an emotional drain. When faced with a crisis in your organization, this is not the kind of cumulative effect you need to watch out for.

In over a hundred instances of speaking with emergency services personnel, I underscore that what they are dealing with is actually repetitive stress. For example, they are confronted with traumatic events on a consistent and regular basis in the line of duty, sometimes in the same day, and they are expected to continue to provide services. Their experiences are a reasonable predictor of what your employees will be going through if they face a widespread traumatic event. The key is for everyone to acknowledge that it is not business as usual when there are multiple tragic events in play. The additive effect of the shocks will have a significant effect on your people.

As an example, consider the healthcare workers in the Greater Toronto Area during the SARS epidemic who faced new and frightening circumstances every single day as they arrived for work. Life in the wake of the 9/11 attacks was similar, as news of colleagues' deaths flowed into organizations, and employees were hit with repeated shocks.

Organizational leaders need to closely monitor the effect of repeated traumas, and be mindful of the fact that people can only handle so much at once.

Send In Additional Troops

Depending on your business location relative to head office, it is often useful to assume that you will not get additional support right away. But one of the most effective and necessary techniques for managing a crisis occurs when an organization can send help. I call them "temporary teams," because they are present only as long as needed. These new recruits can be outside experts hired for particular functions – like food services or laundry – but the most effective examples occur when a team of senior managers assists in the recovery process. I witnessed an example of this approach when I was assisting CIBC in the Cayman Islands. The bank sent a team of senior managers from Toronto – several of them senior VPs – to join the employees who were coping with an actual storm. These leaders immersed themselves in the realities of the post-hurricane destruction to the point of sleeping on the floor with everyone else, and their presence created an incredible sense of loyalty right away and long after the incident.

A temporary team offers a fresh perspective on problems and issues. They arrive rested and healthy, and can take over some of the arduous tasks that the locals have been dealing with. They are also an additional resource for solving the myriad problems that arise, especially when the temporary team is composed of senior officials with the clout to allocate resources for things such as relief funds. Their presence is also helpful in getting clients to accept the capacity limitations that result from the incident.

That said, the main benefit of parachuting a team of senior people into a crisis is that they can serve the local team. Senior executives saying "just tell me what I can do to help you" have a powerful impact on the employees' sense that they are valued. This status reversal can be challenging for newly arrived leaders – especially when the intensity means that the resident employees are short on social graces like please and thank you – but leaders adopting a servant's mindset is crucial. The local employees may sometimes feel off balance with this subordinate approach from people they count on for direction, but a principled, considerate, and interactive style will alleviate any stresses, especially if there are additional supports such as counselling services in place.

Putting senior managers in a position to "roll up their sleeves" and stand elbow to elbow with frontline workers is an incredibly powerful bonding experience for all, and gives leaders a critical opportunity to learn new things and "be there." The more you can get out of the power suit, the more your employees are going to feel connected to you – during the recovery and beyond.

One caution with temporary teams is to remember that their goal is to put themselves out of work. They can never be deemed essential to ongoing recovery. Invariably, the senior people who have come to help will have to get back to their offices, and you do not want their eventual departure to be seen as a loss. This goal is accomplished right from the start by having visiting leaders avoid getting into a position where they are valued more than the existing management team. Every member of the temporary team needs to be helpful but not irreplaceable by adopting a self-effacing approach and turning attention to the local team.

Support Your Managers

It is implicit in the description of temporary teams, but I want to specifically point out the importance of taking care of your managers. Large corporations rely on effective middle management, and this is never more important than in a crisis. When making decisions about resource allocation, establishing priorities, and mapping out directions for the recovery effort, involve your managers as much as you can, and ensure that you have an open conduit for communication. You need to hear from your managers and provide them with essential information. I have seen corporate responses where the well-intentioned efforts of the senior management team to be front and centre led the organization to ignore the managers in the middle. This is a dangerous side effect of leader-centred renewal, and you need to guard against it by actively engaging with your managers and making sure you spend sufficient time supporting their efforts and meeting their needs.

When dealing with the impact of Hurricane Katrina, the P&G employees sought direction and support from the company right away because they had faith in the management. The senior leaders invested Tom Spedding and the team on the ground in New Orleans with the powers they needed to take care of the employees. Tom then empowered and guided the HR manager who was working on site in New Orleans – to the point that he was not needed on the ground during the response.

> There were no obstacles in our chain of command where people were questioning whether we should be doing what we did. There was total unanimity on "let's do the right thing." Cost was the last thing we considered. We were conscious of it, but we didn't let it drive our decision making. Those of us involved were given the responsibility and authority to make some decisions, and we did not have to go all the way to the top to get permission. People trusted that we were going to do the right thing, and there was a sense of autonomy in that. As a result, we were able to get the plant back up and running quickly. Because we were able to do that, we did not lose market share to our competitors, and we were able to cover the costs of the response. If we don't have Folgers to sell to Walmart or Kmart or Kroger, our competitors won't waste time taking that shelf space, and it will be very difficult for us to get that back. Not having our business interrupted for a long time was to our advantage. Yes, it cost money to take care of people on the front end, but it paid dividends for us, because the recovery process was a shared project for the company and the employees.
>
> It's a lesson about the importance of senior management trusting the people who are managing the response. If we had to stop and run every decision up five or six levels of hierarchy before we did any-thing, we would have never gotten anything done, and we would not have had a timely response. This is partly helped by having good plans in place so that a lot of the key issues are sorted out in advance in terms of who is going to do what, for example when it comes to behavioural health response or CISD [critical incident stress debrief-ing] or whatever. I was empowered to make those decisions so that I didn't have to go to my boss and then that boss would go to the next boss. I was able to just use good judgment and make timely decisions, and work with the people who were on the ground in New Orleans and dealing with the crisis.

LEADERSHIP SUMMARY

Key Concept
- *Be prepared to make tough decisions*: soon after the incident, assess the losses and launch your plans with a firm commitment to making the difficult decisions about resource allocation and actions to support employees.

Techniques
- *Allocate your people to non-homogenous teams*: assign people to teams based on their instincts and talents, and establish new working groups to take advantage of the creativity that flows from innovative groupings.
- *Deal with simple problems to solve complex issues*: break large issues into parts to address one at a time so that people feel a sense of control, progress, and perspective.
- *Be open to learning and new ways of thinking*: approach decision making with a heightened commitment to new ideas and perspectives so that you can address novel problems with novel solutions.
- *Keep track of people's emotional means*: constantly assess and monitor the emotional state of your team so that you know how they are handling the recovery effort.
- *Watch for repeated traumas*: be aware that when additional shocks occur, people will be less able to deal with them because they are already compromised by the initial incident.
- *Send in additional troops*: wherever possible, allocate new team members to support those managing the crisis so that new ideas, energy, and perspectives can assist in the process.
- *Support your managers*: focus on providing the frontline leaders with as much information, authority, and support as you can so that they can optimize the site- and situation-specific crisis response.

Chapter Eight

Stage Three: After the Wind Dies Down

I have a responsibility to the worker, both blue-collar and white-collar. I have an equal responsibility to the community. It would have been unconscionable to put 3,000 people on the streets and deliver a deathblow to the cities of Lawrence and Methuen. Maybe on paper our company is worthless to Wall Street, but I can tell you it's worth more.

> Aaron Feuerstein, third-generation owner and CEO of Malden
> Mills in Lawrence, Massachusetts, on investing $25 million
> of his personal money into the business for employees'
> salaries after their plant burned to the ground in December 1995

Key Concept: Carefully Manage Employees' Return to Work

One of the most significant and people-focused techniques I suggest is a staged approach to restoring production. Businesses that proceed slowly and follow their employees' lead set themselves up for long-term success, while those that do not see the need for stages can damage their operations, limit their employees' ability to re-engage with work, and hinder the recovery process. Leaders should assume there will be an extended period of downtime following the crisis when production is either very low or completely stalled.

Leaders can then proceed to work through the three phases of a return to production that I suggest: 1) progressive re-entry, which creates the ideal conditions for employees to return to the company;

2) return to work (RTW), which allows employees to control the rate with which they get back to their positions; and 3) return to productivity (RTP), which is the phrase I use for the overall goal of reestablishing production to ideal levels in a holistic fashion.

Progressive re-entry: When your organization has been through a disaster that damaged homes, destroyed the company's resources, and left people dislocated and disoriented, it is essential to find ways for people to just reconnect to the organization without worrying about having to produce. Human beings need time to transition from the stress of basic needs to the demands of productive work. Look for opportunities to bring employees together in groups on site without expecting much of them. Give people a chance to offer to help out on weekends to deal with physical damage or to provide emotional support to one another. When employees can make decisions about how they help with the recovery, they have an opportunity to set the pace of their re-engagement with the work. They can also begin to think about the larger issues the company is facing without the added stress of having to cope with being immediately productive.

Giving people the time they need to reconnect mentally is helpful. When workers are allowed to do this, camaraderie builds in the employee group, and bonds grow between people from different levels of the organization. The emotional effect of working together on simple things like sorting through rubble is immediate and lasting, because shared experiences are essential for people to connect. I have seen the mood and energy of a workforce change from despair to elation when doing something simple and physical together. Smiles and lightness in their voices were evident as workers headed off at the end of a productive day. This kind of "work" is a highly effective antidote to the stress that overwhelming and frightening conditions create.

When you are managing a re-entry process, there are several specific issues to look for. If some workers were evacuated or chose to leave while others stayed to manage the site through the crisis, there can be tension when those employees return. When I was advising

CIBC in the Cayman Islands, the workers who had stayed throughout the storm were resentful when their colleagues returned. It is easy to see why. They had been through an intense and dangerous situation, and now those who had retreated to safety and security were coming in to help rebuild the company. Resentment may lead to treatment of the returning workers with a degree of contempt. In addition, the people who left may feel a sense of guilt at not having been there for the others. These situations are loaded with emotion, and you need to acknowledge the feelings, validate what people are experiencing, and emphasize the need to move forward together. Re-entry is also a time to monitor closely for an opportunity to remind everyone about the rules of conduct. A post-crisis context is highly chaotic, and there is real value in reconnecting people to the basic rules of conduct. Crises promote uncertainty and confusion, and the more you can introduce stability through structure and safety, the more people can focus on the task at hand and move the company towards productivity.

Return to work: When employees come back to work and immediately try to achieve a 100 per cent effort – whether it is by their choice or at the prompting of the company – their ability to maintain this pace and productivity is short lived. You cannot rush people, even if they say they can handle it. Structure the return so that employees ease in. Too often, the absence of an effective RTW plan leads to physical, emotional, and psychological damage, and this "re-injury" is costly to the individual and the corporation. Benefits costs, replacement costs, episodic production, and the impact of stops and starts on internal and external customer bases are likely.

As an example, consider what happens when a worker cannot continue, and you have to replace that person with a new employee. I have seen new staffers, overwhelmed by the steep learning curve they face in the post-crisis context, resign soon after they join the firm. It is far better for the organization to help the existing workforce re-establish itself in a stepwise fashion so that experienced employees are in place. This assistance includes helping people maintain their faith in the profession and confidence in themselves – two attitudes that can suffer if the return is too much of a struggle. Disillusioned workers have a negative effect on everyone, and you can avoid this by managing the pace for people. People-focused crisis leadership means remembering that people are not machines that can simply be turned on once the power is reconnected.

When I was counselling hospitals in the wake of the SARS crisis, the occupational health departments in the hospitals created a sense of urgency about how quickly healthcare workers should be getting back to the job. It was viewed as an indicator of success if large numbers of workers could return in a hurry. The rapid return pushed many into stressful situations that led them to apply for short-term disability soon after their return date. On one occasion, these applications included one from an occupational health administrator who was having trouble coping with the stress that her own push for aggressive recovery had on her. As an analogy, think about a person who has just finished a marathon: that person cannot now run the hundred meter dash. Going slowly is essential. Offer altered hours, a buddy system, help with family needs, and a gradual increase in work hours so that people can adjust. I know that these supports add strain to the organization – practically and financially – but the long-term benefits of having healthy and confident workers are significant.

I often suggest that leaders approach their RTW plans as if they are overseeing a high-risk workforce. For organizations managing pilots, police officers, various medical employees, or heavy equipment operators, there is a substantial pressure to offer phased RTW, because employees who are not fit to work pose a significant risk to themselves and others. In these contexts, the organization can expose itself to litigation if it is not careful about bringing people back online slowly. Approaching your own reintegration plans as if your employees are in a high-risk context can help you maintain a people-focused view about the rate of RTW. For some leaders, it may be helpful to think about employee support as similar to that of a physiotherapist working with someone recovering from a major injury. It is essential that the therapist help the patient set an appropriate pace of recovery in order to avoid unnecessary setbacks and ensure consistent healing. In an RTW process, the leader needs to keep track of people's efforts to make sure they are not setting themselves up for failure by trying to solve the whole crisis at once or to perform superhuman acts. People are highly influenced by messaging about "how well we are doing" or "how much we are able to get done today." Sometimes, good news can have a negative impact, because at every level of the company, there is pressure for individuals, departments, and teams to appear as if they are "winning" in the war against the crisis. I sometimes have to help leaders see that the old "get back on the horse" mindset is highly dangerous. Only a leader can reassure workers that moving slowly is an acceptable and necessary way to approach their RTW. By controlling employees' workloads and monitoring their progress – emotionally, physically, and mentally – leaders can ensure success. Wherever possible, encourage small and manageable steps so you avoid setting people up with tasks that they will not be able to manage. Failures, no matter how small, will add to people's sensation that they are not good enough. Increasing workloads needs to be managed so that confidence can drive the RTW process.

If you manage the RTW properly, the benefits will be substantial. Your people will feel respected, trusted, and valued. They will believe that they are your priority and not merely a means to an end. This view will increase retention and loyalty from them and also from their families, who will view the company as playing an active role in taking care of their loved one. There is also a long-term benefit, because the company's reputation for taking care of its people will grow, making recruitment efforts easier and more effective long after the storm has passed. In general, hold an image in mind of workers recovering from an earthquake that destroyed their company and their homes. As they rebuild their homes, they can gradually return to work. Overall, you want to help confidence grow and batteries recharge, and develop a strong sense of connection between the company and employee families.

Return to productivity: Once you have managed the stages of your employees' reconnection with work, have a vision for your RTP goals. At heart, this is about knowing how to measure current production, which requires a significant shift in mindset. If you compare current production to the pre-crisis levels, you create unrealistic expectations for everyone and allow a sense of failure to infest the culture. All forward motion should be considered a success. The rate of production on any given day during a crisis recovery can only be compared with the previous day. The leadership needs to constantly trumpet small, incremental increases and resist any temptation to let people's hopes grow too big. Too many times, I have seen organizations work wonders in their direct management of crisis conditions, only to fall into the trap of wanting to run before they can walk with their RTP plan.

The negative side effects of rushing to full productive capacity are significant. Managers are wise to do their best impersonation of Scarlett O'Hara and say, "I'll think of that tomorrow," because trying to do too much at once leads to breakdowns in machines, people, and communication. If you rush, product quality may suffer, and you risk a negative reaction from your clients. You will also see loyalty from employees plummet, resignations and terminations increase, general absenteeism rise, and a degree of "working absence" develop, where workers are physically present but not mentally or emotionally engaged and are underperforming. Add to this that employees will be under pressure from their families to look for a new job if they feel that the company has unrealistic expectations.

Successful RTP plans – like the ones I have seen in place at P&G and CIBC – set a pace that takes care of employees, even when the employees themselves don't know what they need. In particular, rushing can also lead to production paralysis, which occurs when an organization is forced to shut down operations after it becomes evident that the production demands the leaders have put in place are not sustainable. When this happens, the emotional climate becomes toxic. Managers can develop a degree of hesitation about asking employees to get back to work that borders on embarrass-ment, and staff end up with nothing they can count on to help build their self-esteem. People need to be productive, and small successes are far better than none at all. Frozen production causes managers and workers alike to spiral into a loss of confidence in the corpora-tion, their colleagues, and themselves. This outlook then dominates people's thinking, with nothing to provide a sense of progress or success over the adverse conditions.

As you move through the phases, maintain your focus on people's needs. Start with constant vigilance about the extras you load onto people, and measure productivity and success based on what indi-viduals can personally handle. Every person is different in terms of coping skills, work history, personal support system, and goals. Your overall goal cannot be just getting everyone back to work. It has to be getting everyone back to healthy, productive, engaged, and viable work. Set the production targets based on the reality of your people, and remember that the more devastating the crisis has been, the longer and more incremental the RTW process needs to be. Also keep in mind that this kind of staged increase in production is not just for individuals. Different departments and divisions of the company will need customized goal setting, particularly if an entire department has been hit hard by the crisis. Dysfunctional people cannot support each other. In some cases, you will need to separate the members of a department and spread them out in other areas of the company to ensure that those employees can get the support they need with the reintegration.

When the core leadership team uses goal setting that celebrates small increases in productivity and establishes realistic targets, workers feel inspired and energized, which offsets the disorientat-ing state following an event. I talk to leaders about the "3 Vs" of goals: visualize it, verbalize it, and value it. If you can provide tangi-ble and realistic daily goals, publish those targets for all to see, and collectively celebrate when they are achieved, morale will improve. Everyone will be able to connect what they are doing to the overall success of the company. Procter & Gamble was brilliant at this after the earthquake in Turkey. The corporation began slowly and set its expectations for production as low as possible. Senior managers posted their goals every day and did not compare the results to the pre-earthquake numbers. They created a culture in which everyone arrived each day ready to do a bit better than the day before. Workers believed that the company was committed to the incremental approach and felt valued and capable. From line workers to secretaries to senior executives, everyone knew that P&G was moving forward.

Finally, consider which departments and divisions you will bring online first. Focus on the aspects of your business and the people responsible for establishing financial stability for the company right away, and assign resources to that part of the operation. I lived through this with CIBC in the Cayman Islands when the bank chose to get the mutual fund division up and running again while leaving the trust funds on hold. This meant putting IT, staff, telephones, and electricity to work in that part of the business. It was the same kind of prioritizing that happened at Cantor Fitzgerald following the 9/11 attacks. The company focused on the parts of its financial services that would help stabilize it. You can establish these priorities as part of the ongoing impact assessments you conduct.

P&G is particularly effective at managing staged returns to work. It has learned from experience that a slow approach that allows individuals to make decisions about how to get back into their jobs is best in the long run. Recalling the recovery from Katrina, Tom Spedding stated:

> It was about two weeks before the water receded enough to get into the plant. All we were able to do prior to that were flyovers to take pictures and try to assess the damage. After about three weeks, we had about a third of our plant population living in the trailers, and they were the first group of people who went into the plant once it was accessible. When we eventually got into the plant and started to get back to production, we worked very slowly to increase it. We started at 10 per cent of capacity and increased it as slowly as possible for

people over the course of a few weeks. It was around eight weeks after we were able to get back in there that the plant was back up to 100 per cent capacity.

Techniques for After the Crisis

Keep the Identity of the Company in Mind

It may seem odd to suggest that maintaining a sense of corporate identity in a crisis is important, but I have seen the benefits for companies that do. Every company has a distinct culture, personality, and product, and everything you do during a crisis should be consistent with what the company stands for. The approach you take will set the tone for interactions with your employees, but it will also make a significant impression on your customers – especially in the period of time immediately following the event. Avoid becoming like the businesses you are competing against. Don't create a situation in which your customers start to think of you as a lesser version of another firm. Making decisions based on the character of your own firm is critical, even bold ones that involve a degree of risk. When you are off balance, it is easy to copy what is happening elsewhere, but a paint-by-numbers approach is only going to undermine your long-term prospects for success. I have seen many organizations take advantage of the possibilities for change post-crisis to energize the staff, policies, products, and services in innovative ways. It is a unique opportunity to redefine and renew.

The benefits of attending to corporate identity are substantial, as Bonnie Adamson explains about her approach to rebuilding North York General Hospital when the crisis was over.

After SARS, NYGH was filled with anger, frustration, despair, and a great sense of loss. From a leadership CEO perspective, it was a unique – once-in-a-lifetime – opportunity to rebuild an organization. We undertook a culture/leadership transformation and created a positive culture of safety, empowerment, accountability, and learning.

It took several years to engage and empower all the NYGH family, but alignment and community were achieved. Leaders were developed to demonstrate a collaborative, engaging style, and state-of-the-art infection prevention and control was achieved. Many lessons were learned both at NYGH and across the entire system, especially that preparedness for disasters was an imperative. The outstanding achievement by NYGH staff, physicians, and volunteers has been sustained now eleven years later. NYGH has received multiple awards for patient safety, high quality of care/service, and healthy work environment.

Be Prepared for Aftershocks

While in Turkey working with P&G, I was meeting with a team of senior managers to check on the recovery when the building began to shake. Panicked, we all ran for doorways – the typical response to an earthquake. Only it wasn't an earthquake. It was an aftershock. Seismographers will tell you that following a large quake, the earth's plates continue to settle, sending out tremors that are highly similar to the original event. People who have just lived through the big quake react to these minor tremors with panic because their brains tell them that the whole thing is happening again. Since then, the concept of an aftershock has been a metaphor I use to help leaders comprehend the emotional climate they are working within after an incident. Any number of situations can act as a "trigger" for an emotional memory, and the reaction will launch people back into the extreme state they experienced during the incident, like a war veteran reacting to a backfiring motorcycle. From bad press about the organization to changes in leadership to gossip and other sources of insecurity, any number of inciting incidents can have a disproportionate emotional effect on employees, especially if there is a physical stimulus like a shaking building or a plane flying too low.

Like many of the effects I have illustrated in this book, the "aftershock" can happen at the departmental, divisional, or corporate level, because collectives are just large groups of people. Some examples of this effect include workers in New York reacting when there were threats of additional terrorist attacks following 9/11, hospitals in Toronto hit hard by the anniversary of the SARS incident, and bad press about North York General Hospital sending a ripple of falling confidence through the staff. News and events that would have been easily ignored before the crisis take on a whole new emotional context – much greater than might be expected. It's like a family with teenaged children. Under normal circumstances, there is likely to be some bickering and arguing, but a family dealing with an extreme emotional trauma can create internal conflict at a whole different level.

Act Quickly While People Are Fluid

Because business leaders are not generally therapists and counsellors, they may not be familiar with a human quality important to remember in a crisis: people take time to integrate new states of being. In my experience, there is a time-sensitive window of opportunity immediately following the event during which a long-term relationship with the crisis can be altered and improved if you provide a structured context for the emotion of the event. This compressed time period explains why I am often on a plane shortly after the phone rings. Just like steel workers who have a short window for pouring liquid steel into a mould, the organization has a critical period during which to help workers with the various beliefs, patterns, and habits that they will have in the post-crisis world. The sooner you can put the support in place, the better.

Keep Communicating

Maintain your link to employees long after the breakneck news cycle has eased: be the source of information and squash rumours. Leave your command centre up and running for some time, continue to hold information sessions, maintain the employee family liaison position, listen to employee questions about whatever is on their minds, and talk to them about the arc of the recovery process. I have seen companies that have managed the communication brilliantly during the incident close the channels too soon and allow negativity and confusion to infect the post-crisis climate. Keep talking to employees about whatever comes up: information about the incident itself, about helping services, about business re-engagement, or about issues that employees and their families are facing. This continuing contact is especially important if there is any possibility of more bad news coming out, such as updates on the health status of colleagues who were injured in the incident.

Bonnie Adamson and her team illustrated the importance of this approach in the short break between SARS outbreaks.

> At the end of the first wave of the crisis (SARS I), we focused on debriefing the experience. Through surveys and conversations, feedback from the staff perspective during the first phase began to describe how difficult and fearful it had been for our people. Some of my observations during this period included the diversity in leadership styles. Some leaders would boss people around or attempt to make unilateral decisions in a situation where the goal was joint decision making. They were displaying what they thought was great leadership – making tough decisions unilaterally in the time of a crisis. There is definitely a place for decisiveness in a crisis at certain times in certain roles, but not in team decision-making processes. I observed which leaders demonstrated good project management skills and those requiring assistance. Of note was that some leaders had difficulty following through on commitments and understanding the accountability of their role. At times, one would see a leader showing an attitude that if you did not do something, no one would notice. The comparison between a lack of execution by some and the super overachievers on the other hand was fascinating to watch – but very stressful to manage.

Provide Mental and Emotional Support Long After the Incident

Assume that people will be coping with the event for a long time after it has faded into memory. Ensure that the mental health supports you put in place immediately are extended as workers transition to the long-term task of managing the effects of the crisis. You can do this by having the EAP professionals you hired come back and check in with your team. You should also ensure that your whole senior management team attend reasonably regular debriefing sessions where they talk about the stresses of the incident and the recovery process. Leaders are especially prone to a "just get on with it" attitude, which can set them up for a stress-induced collapse later on. I also advise companies to promote non-official healing through memorial services and the recognition of anniversaries. People take time to heal, and in many cases need reassurance that the long-term emotional impact is totally normal by seeing other people equally affected.

LEADERSHIP SUMMARY

Key Concept
- *Carefully manage employees' return to work*: have a staged process for employees to resume working that empowers them to control their own pace, gives them time to adjust and have small successes, and respects the slow nature of emotional recovery.

Techniques
- *Always keep the identity of the company in mind*: make decisions consistent with the culture and values of the organization so that employees and customers alike can believe in the organization and relate to its identity on a long-term basis.
- *Watch for aftershocks*: accept that there will be ongoing emotional recoil for your people.
- *Act quickly while people are fluid*: put emotional and social supports in place right away so that employees can process the confusion, loss, and grief in a proactive fashion that will set them up for long-term healing.

- *Keep communicating*: ensure that you continue to connect through information sharing long after the main event is over.
- *Provide mental and emotional support after the incident*: put in place and maintain EAP and counselling support as long as possible, based on the recognition that emotional coping takes time.

Chapter Nine

Stage Four: When the Quiet Finally Comes

Life can only be understood backwards; but it must be lived forwards.

Søren Kierkegaard

Key Concept: Ensure a Proper, Collaborative Reflection Process

As indicated earlier, I view crisis leadership as happening in four stages. The final stage, reflection, is essential to building a solid foundation for the future. It is also a critical part of the long-term healing. The methods you use for dealing with the "content" of crises are often the same methods you can use to deal with the emotion. This is why creating a collaborative business continuity plan has dual benefits, and also why all organizations should implement a shared and integrated approach to debriefing the good, bad, and ugly of how it was all handled.

Done properly, shared reflection can be very effective for team building and emphasizing corporate culture and identity. It's a time when you come together as a community and say, "This is what we are, this is what we did well, and this is how we value each other." In my work with companies, reflection mostly occurs when the "it's over" indicators arrive: production has reached a predictable and reliable level, the financial status of the company has stabilized, and employees are reasonably settled into routines. You want to be far enough removed from the incident so that people are not reliving the raw emotion of the events, but you also want to make sure that the reflection process happens soon enough to be meaningful.

I have sometimes worked hard to help corporate leaders see the importance of reflection. Their hesitance is reasonable: they have finally got the organization on track, they have spent a significant amount of time and money managing throughout the crisis, and their world seems pretty settled. The last thing they want to do is churn it all up again and allocate time and resources to revisiting the difficulties they faced. They are also hesitant to draw attention to their failings. We are all keen to avoid public embarrassment. In the face of these concerns, I emphasize the forces that are at work under the surface of the post-crisis organization. First, there is an incredible opportunity for clarity, growth, and renewal in shared reflection. Having so much rich content to discuss is rare, and wise organizational leaders don't miss an opportunity to take advantage of that moment. Second, I warn leaders to keep the concept of repetitive patterns in mind. Without reflection and a concerted attempt to assess the organization's response to the crisis, the weaknesses that were in place during the crisis will recur when any degree of challenge presents itself. Like alcoholism that passes down through generations, ineffective administrative practices are perpetuated if no one stops the cycle. Consider the national amnesia that can lead an entire country into a similar set of decisions and actions if there has not been a sufficient process of identifying, integrating, and recording the historical lessons. Churchill's famous urging to "Study History!" isn't an empty call for more book learning; it's a call to learn from the past in order to control the future. Crisis reflection is also an incredible way to formally celebrate successes, because remembering and recording what went right is as important as seeing and adjusting for errors. In essence, I try to help leaders see that taking a "time heals" approach is short sighted. Active and deliberate reflection is key.

The central method of shared reflection I recommend is a wagon wheel review. The process involves bringing in neutral facilitators to organize a structured review of all aspects of the crisis response

Figure 9.1 Sample Wagon Wheel Structure

in all areas of the company. I call it a "wagon wheel review" because I encourage companies to set up a central group that consists of the senior management team, and then establish "hubs" in each of the key areas of the organization.

To illustrate, I have included a diagram of how a wagon wheel review might be organized in a healthcare setting.

In some cases, the management team is the "axle" of the whole wagon wheel system. Each spoke radiating from this main axle terminates in a "hub," each of which represents one of the central departments or divisions or any type of groupings participating in the review. Each of these hubs then radiates spokes that represent the subcommittees – however many are needed to ensure a comprehensive review.

Subcommittees can be established in parallel with the functions and departments that exist already, but it can be useful to organize the review around the groups that were active during the crisis. It is also a good idea to have the customers represented, in whatever form is relevant to your organization, so that you ensure consultation and involvement of all stakeholders. Once the various working groups have been established, each should work through a structured review of the response and feed information into the hub for the eventual change plan. The wagon wheel review structure ensures that the meetings and eventual documentation reflect everyone's ideas about how the crisis was handled and that employees feel a sense of ownership and connection to the company. If the report that comes out of a wagon wheel review reflects what employees are really thinking, it will energize the company. While it can be difficult for leaders to see their failings and errors in print, nothing galvanizes a company more than an authentic and honest conversation about what happened. People are so used to marketing speak and hollow language that accurate and genuine communication resonates deeply and builds loyalty and commitment.

Techniques for a Wagon Wheel Review

Establish a Structure and Ground Rules

Establishing a structure for the review is critical. In the absence of facilitating forces and rules of engagement that ensure genuine reflection and prescription, the reflection process will fall apart. Common among these potential difficulties is that employees with an axe to grind can dominate and overemphasize particular issues that bothered them. This kind of narrow and localized focus is detrimental and needs to be avoided. There are procedures to address this tendency. Ensure that the debriefing sessions are facilitated by a neutral party. People are more open to questions and clarifications from someone they do not perceive to be invested in the outcome. It simply does not work to have the department head chair that teams' meeting. Employees will not be open and honest, and the department head will not be able to effectively engage them. Professional facilitators help people to reframe and articulate their ideas in positive and accurate language. They are also beneficial because employees have no relationship with them beyond the process. This allows the procedural necessities – like having meetings start and end on time – to occur without any hint of personal affront. People are hypersensitive to being heard and valued. If they feel that the facilitator is simply following the rules when he or she suggests that the meeting wrap up, there is less risk of anger and frustration. It is also important to remember that facilitating this kind of review is complicated. Even the most dynamic and engaging leaders don't necessarily have the skills required to get people to talk openly. By engaging outside experts, you ensure an ideal review.

Once the wagon wheel structure is in place and the facilitators are identified, the initial task is to establish ground rules, which should be outlined in advance of the meetings. Some of the general rules I suggest are as follows:

1. All members have an equal voice, and there is no hierarchy in the meetings that makes one person's view more important or valuable than another.
2. The review is not a personal process but concerns the needs and experiences of the team and the organization.
3. All positive and negative outcomes will be observed, recorded, and understood.
4. The meetings are not a forum for attacks on services, leaders, or departments.
5. Personal offence cannot be the entry point for receiving feedback about how things went.
6. All feedback is welcome and useful.
7. An emphasis on an objective and precise interpretation of the events is critical.
8. The meetings are strictly confidential.

This last rule is necessary because the kinds of conversations that take place during the review can be juicy fuel for gossip if there are not explicit expectations around confidentiality. It is crucial to maintain that trust, so I encourage organizations to have people sign an agreement that they will keep the conversations inside the room.

Focus on Shared Healing and Learning

With basic guidelines in place – and emphasized at the beginning of each meeting – the overall goal needs to be publicized broadly. All employees must accept that the spirit of the reflection process is to help the organization heal and grow, and that the emphasis is on the "common good" of the company and all stakeholder groups. From there, the procedure should be focused on sharing ideas and assessing strengths and weaknesses. I recommend that groups use the timeline of the crisis as a guide for discussions, because remembering events and procedures in sequence ensures that nothing will be missed and tends to prompt robust memories. It is also a natural way of connecting various parts together because it emphasizes the actual cause–effect sequence. Make sure members who join the evaluation teams at the beginning stay throughout the review: fragmented or incomplete reviews are ineffective and lack integrity. The cohesion of the group – especially the commitment to objective and open conversation – takes time to establish, and the members need time to get to know each other in that context. Logistically, review the guidelines regularly and advertise the timing of meetings widely so that the process is manageable and people don't feel offended if a given meeting has to proceed without them or cannot extend beyond its assigned time. I also promote adherence to fixed timelines so that the subcommittees can complete their work in a timely fashion, which allows the hub committees positioned at the axle of the wagon wheel to begin sorting and organizing the volume of material that is coming in. An extended delay between the meetings and the production of the report is not healthy. The only way that a significant review can be completed on a time budget, especially in a large organization, is for the leadership and the facilitators to work hard at protecting the timeline. The review has to be a priority or it will not happen – at least not in a fashion that ensures effective learning across the organization.

With these basic rules and procedures in place, the work of the committees can begin. The essential focus of the meetings needs to be on detail and precision, but the two broad questions that underlie the entire process are 1) How did we do? and 2) What could we have done differently? These main inquiries can then be supported by sequences of questions that act like dominoes, exploring increasingly detailed layers:

1. In what way did we perform well or poorly?
2. When was this particular issue evident?
3. What would it take to do it differently next time?
4. What resources might have changed the outcome?
5. How could we have supported people more effectively?
6. What was the effect of that situation?
7. What impact did the effect have on employees, management, and customers?

The end goal is to work towards recommendations. All the subcommittees and central hubs are working towards a set of suggestions for changes that can make the company stronger. This is the part that engrains the learning in the corporation's memory. Each subcommittee's recommendations are represented at the central hub by the leader of that group. That leader then reports back to the subgroup about how the information was received by the central committee. Any suggestions made by subgroups should be realistic, accurate, and in tune with the organization's limitations. The facilitators, managers, and employees all need to have a "reality check" in place to make sure that what they suggest can actually work. Highly unrealistic plans for improvement force the management of the company to dismiss the suggestions as untenable. This is not a good dynamic.

Create a Corporate Change Initiative Plan

Once all the recommendations have been delivered to the various hub committees, the management team has the daunting challenge of prioritizing and assessing them on its way to creating a corporate change initiative plan (CCIP). This part of the process mirrors that of budgeting or developing strategic plans. It is critical and highly complex. I emphasize that no matter what is included in the report, there needs to be accurate, open, and complete feedback to the subgroups about all the recommendations, whether or not they are included in the final change plan. Employees know that management have difficult decisions to make and that everything isn't possible, but they need an explanation or the wheels of rumour and speculation – and the attendant hostility – will begin to turn. It really is the case that sufficient time for questions or clarifications helps people accept the decisions that have been made and elevates trust and engagement. It also helps if the bulk of the recommendations can at least make it into the plan. Even recording goals for change that might take five years to implement is better than cutting recommendations completely.

Once established, the CCIP is a catalyst for action as the recommendations become goals for every area of the company, empowering departmental leaders and their teams to bring them to life. When the resources are provided to implement plans that many people were involved in creating, there is a surge of energy and connection throughout the organization. While implementing the recommendations, remember to keep the wagon wheel committees in place. These groups can provide a sense of stability during the review. People manage changes more easily when they can count on their review group to ensure that their voice is being heard. Overall, the key is to initiate changes and proceed through the implementation of the plan with an approach that emphasizes communication, connection, and confidence.

The NAV CANADA critical incident peer team is one of the strongest corporate employee and family support teams I have encountered, because it is open to change and improvement. For the organization and its peer support team, the post-incident assessment process has allowed NAV CANADA to develop their large-scale events training and personal issues training, and the company has benefited from this education and preparation. As Lyne Wilson pointed out:

> When the crisis in Moncton ended, we conducted a review with the employees and managers within the Moncton Air Traffic Control Centre. In so doing, we were able to see practices and procedures that we wanted to replicate in the future if we had to respond to another regional crisis. While doing the review, we were acutely aware that the nature of the aviation industry means we have to be ready for crises of this size and also on a larger scale, involving more people and potential loss of life.

Organizations such as NAV CANADA that are charged with public safety responsibilities have an immediate need to restore business to its pre-crisis stable state. A strong structure is required in order to guarantee that both the restoration and the public safety goals are achieved expeditiously. There must also be a well-trained peer support team that fully understands the magnitude and impact of a large-scale event linked to the corporate emergency preparedness plan. These are integral components to the stabilization of the employees, their families, and ultimately the business.

Procter & Gamble also has a highly sophisticated approach to reflection in the wake of a crisis. As Tom Spedding explained:

> I think that our experience in Kobe, Japan, was a big learning moment for the company, when we took the time to do an after-action review properly. It was the first natural disaster that I had experienced, even though I had been with P&G for a long time. It was a huge event where thousands of lives were impacted, and we were really worried about a mass exodus where our people would conclude that they needed to get out of there and that they didn't care about P&G and

they were going home. In Kobe, we targeted family members, because many times the employees were so busy, and if we could support their spouses and children, help to make them comfortable, then life could get back to normal and the workers could know that their family was okay so that they have one less thing to worry about. If you ignore the spouse, you can lose the employee. We also learned that parents' primary concern is about their kids, so the kids became a big focus because many of them were traumatized because the earthquake happened in the middle of the night and threw them out of their beds. Kids were having trouble sleeping, were wetting their beds, and were behaving differently. Parents had to decide how to cope with all of that, and one of the answers that was highly appealing for them was to go back to their home country. If they had done that, we would have had to rebuild the business, and it would have taken much longer than it did to get back to normal. So supporting employees and their families became the centre point of our crisis response plans.

In particular, P&G has specific protocols that are used for review:

After an event, we do an after-action analysis to identify what we learned, what we did well, and what we didn't do so well, and the plans come from that process. I think it is a military term. We get the key people who were involved together, and we talk about what happened. It usually takes a few days to do it, but it can spread over a few weeks because we often don't have the luxury of getting everyone into the same room.

In Halifax, Nancy Tower was involved in an extensive review to improve Nova Scotia Power's state of emergency preparedness.

We have since developed an emergency services restoration plan (ESRP), which we have used a number of times and which we test regularly. We all learned a lot from the experience, and now we have an ESRP that we test regularly. It is structured. For example, I am the storm lead – the storm boss. That's my role. I'm in our emergency operations centre, and I'm the lead of what is now a large group. During our drills, we talk about how things would unfold in a crisis. We talk about how many crews to bring in and for how long. We talk about how long it can be before the power is restored. And how much extra help we need to bring in. We also explore ways that we can use advanced weather tracking systems to get out in front of storms. It is an interesting process.

LEADERSHIP SUMMARY

Key Concept
- *Engage in a wagon wheel review process*: ensure proper, collaborative reflection to help individuals, groups, and the entire organization learn from the incident, make changes, and continue to heal.

Techniques
- *Hire outside facilitators*: use unbiased experts to create a safe and fair process.
- *Use a structured process to ensure effective reflection*: be deliberate and careful in the review so that employees understand what is happening, and all key steps occur.
- *Have established ground rules*: ensure that all participants understand how the reflection process works, and create clear guidelines for how input should be managed, expressed, and collected.
- *Create a corporate change initiative plan (CCIP)*: work towards a written report that outlines all required changes with timelines and responsibilities clearly identified for all employees to read and share.
- *Engage teams in making the changes they have suggested*: empower individuals and teams to apply the recommendations they make so that the change process is sensitive to the needs of each area.

- *Keep the wagon wheel committees in place for some time*: maintain the review committees long after the majority of the changes have been made so that there is a sense of stability and continuity for your employees.
- *Ensure that people who join the review committees stay on them*: select the members of the committees based on their ability to stay with the process so they are a constant presence during the recovery effort.

Part Three

Leadership Lessons

Chapter Ten

Lessons for the Daily Storm

I can hear your whisper and distant mutter. I can smell your damp on the breeze and in the sky I see the halo of your violence. Storm I know you are coming.

Robert Fanney

The people I have met through my work, including those who are the focus of this book, live in the constant storm of everyday leadership issues. Real leaders operate from an interior force that guides them in times of confusion, panic, and fear. They are the people who say, "This is what we need to do," when no one else can, and whose confidence and clarity become the foundation for action.

Most organizations never face the large-scale damage and disaster that a hurricane or a shooting can bring, but many situations and issues that leaders deal with regularly could easily be described as crises. I suggested that a crisis could be characterized as a time when the *unexpected and complex dominate, and when instability, damage, threat, and risk to the company and its people are the norm.* This type of situation may be what leaders face on any day the moment someone comes through their door. Managers are people who deftly supervise routines, sometimes on a very large scale. Leaders are people you seek when you have a mess on your hands and don't know what to do. When we need someone to bring certainty to an uncertain situation, to give confidence when fear dominates, to offer stability when the world is off balance, or to see the solution in the centre of something incredibly complex, we turn to a leader. No matter the size of the issues that we face, leaders are the ones who guide us through the storms of daily life.

Consider two descriptions of leadership. The first is from former secretary of state Colin Powell, a retired four-star general from the US Army: "Leadership is solving problems. The day soldiers stop bringing you their problems is the day you have stopped leading them. They have either lost confidence that you can help or concluded you do not care. Either case is a failure of leadership." Powell's comment is typically interpreted as a version of the old adage about looking over your shoulder to see if people are still following you. That is a reasonable view. But to me, the central idea is solving problems. Powell points out that leadership is about helping people with issues they cannot sort out for themselves. Leaders have to find creative responses to messy situations.

Now consider the notion of creativity when Michael McKinney, president of M2 Communications, writes: "So much of what a leader does cannot be objectively measured. To reduce leadership to a set of algorithms is to remove it from its context; to ignore the complexities, the contradictions, and the possibilities. Artists must deal with uncertainty, contradictions and diversity almost by definition. Leaders need to have this capacity."[1] McKinney is partly suggesting that leadership is a kind of alchemy or magic that cannot be distilled into a formula. It is a lovely idea, and there is truth in it. But what resonates for me is the description of what artists and leaders work with: uncertainty, contradictions, and diversity. His phrasing is similar to the words I use to define a crisis.

If we accept that every day is, in spirit, an exercise in crisis management – which complexity-hardened leaders in any context would certainly support – we can then think about the themes that have emerged in this exploration of crisis leadership and draw some core lessons that can be of use to those who face "the daily storm."

Lesson #1: Be Human

Throughout this book, I have emphasized the importance of creating a climate that removes barriers to authentic interaction. This has to begin with a leader who is committed to being real. Leaders who sit in front of their team and adopt mannerisms, a tone of voice, or an overall quality that says, "This is how a leader looks," create distance and alienate their followers. Most charismatic leaders assert their status as a person instead of projecting a face of power. Being a leader always requires moments of formality and decorum, but the best leaders I have seen have a way of being themselves no matter what the setting or circumstance. They speak with a personal tone and exude genuineness, helping everyone around them feel the warmth of their humanity. They instinctively know that workers connect to the person first and to the organization or cause second. Even when they are very different from the workers in culture or background, a strong connection can be developed through authentic interactions. I have seen many examples of leaders who are soft spoken, quirky, or peculiar in some way, but because they are committed to being themselves, they have the loyalty and support of their followers.

Being yourself requires confidence and knowing how to interact informally with people. Great leaders often share personal anecdotes from their lives, such as funny childhood memories or a story from their morning commute. They also have a strong sense of their own tendencies and talk about how those habits influence actions and decisions. They are good at admitting when they have made an error and often use self-deprecating humour very effectively, especially when they joke about something that everyone is thinking. Effective leaders tend to approach interactions with an open and informal tone, even when they are in a highly formal setting or need to establish professional distance from others.

Overall, effective leaders are highly approachable and leave people feeling that they are easy to talk to. These habits seem to flow from an acceptance of self, making these leaders the kind of people who don't have any illusions about how they are doing and what they are all about.

From what I have seen, effective leaders arrive at this state after a great deal of life experience and self-assessment. They have been in a variety of contexts that have helped them appreciate their own strengths, and they actively reflect on their experiences. They also surround themselves with friends and colleagues who are both brutally honest and incredibly insightful. They are deeply committed to their relationships with friends and family, and within their community and workplace, because they know that everyone wants to connect.

Over the past fifteen years, I have become increasingly involved with several police services in North America as they cope with the after-effects of tragic events. In the midst of chaos, I have had the rare opportunity to closely observe police leaders and see how they provide support and guidance through events that often involve losing one of their own. One such occurrence was on 13 January 2011.

Sergeant Ryan Russell had been killed the previous day by a snow plow, driven by a man named Richard Kachkar. I was spending the day with Toronto Police Service's Chief Bill Blair and his senior team. Like many of his team members, Chief Blair was devastated. It was evident that he had been deeply hurt by the loss. Chief Blair led his people through the incident with poise and grace, but he did not hide his sadness behind a mask. His commitment to being human first was a fitting example of the way in which effective leaders intuitively understand that people are always the priority.

Lesson #2: Treat People like People

So often, standing with a senior executive in a firm while they talk to an employee, I have been struck by the ease and openness of the conversation. Great leaders talk to people as though there is nothing else in the world that matters in that moment but the interaction. They are interested in the person and regard that person as a unique individual, not a corporate category or object.

It is too easy for leaders to develop a mechanized view of employees. This thinking is really dangerous in an organization because it creates an underlying tone of distrust and distance. Excellent leaders make a concerted effort to spend time with their teams. They listen, laugh, tell stories, share ideas, and engage. They are unfailingly generous and always interested in how people are doing. They build a community where there are no conversations about "company loyalty" because people just take it for granted.

These leaders really enjoy talking to people and look for opportunities to do it at work and in social contexts, such as going for a meal or coffee. They take time to hear about what is happening in the workers' lives. They have running jokes and ongoing topics from the news, sports, or other personal interests. They learn what people like to do, and they remember details about people's lives, such as where an individual worker grew up. They know people's names.

Great leaders leave the impression that they really know people, and that their knowledge has not come in some effort to manage perceptions or play politics. Even in large multinational corporations, where it is impossible for a senior executive to meet everyone, their approach to interactions can still say, "I appreciate you as a person." This quality in great leaders is connected to a commitment to equality. They see everyone as having value: while they know that their own role in the corporation often has greater scope and impact than the role of others, they never think that they are better. From what I have seen, excellent leaders have a long history of living and working in settings where relationships and real human contact is essential. They are students of the human experience. Their interest in people is one of the driving forces behind their commitment to sincere relationships.

A few years ago, I was teaching a group of officers at the Ontario Provincial Police (OPP) headquarters in Orillia, Ontario, when one of the strongest leaders I have ever seen came into my life. Before I began my talk, my OPP contact informed me that the commissioner, Chris Lewis, wanted to address the team for a few minutes. Having conducted more than a hundred lectures a year over twenty-five years in hundreds of organizations, I am used to having a manager, director, vice-president, or CEO address the audience before I begin. Their talks are often impersonal and, even worse, rushed. Most leaders want to get in, do their duty, and get out.

That isn't what Chris Lewis had in mind. He came in with an energy seldom seen in the C-level hallways. His face, body language, and tone of voice conveyed that he was thrilled to be there and couldn't imagine being anywhere else. His approach was energizing and inspiring.

Since then, I have seen Chris engage with people on a regular basis, and I look forward to it every time. To begin with, he will walk into a room and stand in front of officers and civilians who might come from any of the professional disciplines or geographical territories for which his approximately 9,300 employees are responsible, and he often surprises people by knowing their names. Better yet, he will also talk to each person about what is happening where they work or with their spouse, parents, or kids – whose names he often knows. He uses humour, often self-deprecating, to bond with his staff, and always has a story or two from his mental archive to pull out for a quick lesson. He always reminds his troops that he too is a police officer who has done many of the jobs that they are doing. People relate to Chris and feel that their commissioner can relate to them. His approach is authentic, and the results are extraordinary.

In my time working with Chris, I have seen him cope with challenging situations across the spectrum from the political to the tactical to the personal. His bond with his people and emphasis on their needs sets him apart. But what makes Chris's story even more interesting is that early on in his time as a senior leader in the OPP, he had a brain tumour. Undaunted, he fought through the cancer and returned to work, advancing to more and more senior levels of responsibility in the organization. His determination to serve and resilience in getting back to work have shaped his character and commitment. Chris is a man whose commitment to be there for his people through anything and everything is evident.

Lesson #3: Acquire Wisdom and Seek Direction

Leading an organization requires an ability to provide insight, often at high speed, in the face of shifting variables and uncertainties. Leaders have to know how to balance long-term implications with short-term issues, how to consider the big picture without losing track of the small details, and how to assess the degree to which they should be firm or flexible. Great leaders have a knack for making key decisions, focusing on the topics that need to be discussed at any given time, and seeing how the current focus will logically lead to particular outcomes. They can zoom their lens in and out with ease, and they are incredibly knowledgeable about the various parts of their organization. They are calm in a crisis, see into the heart of things, and regularly display sound judgment in the face of complex issues. They are also able to get the relevant information needed to make a good decision and can predict the future based on what they have learned from the past because they do their homework and make the most of every conversation, discussion, or meeting. Great leaders are also certain about what they know and don't know, and engage their teams in a dialogue that enriches their sense of the business and ensures the best approach to their work. In short, they are wise.

This wisdom seems to come with time. The best leaders I have seen have had a great deal of experience in a variety of settings, often beginning at the frontlines of their chosen field. Taking time to get to the top means leaders experience difficult, often brutal, jobs and situations that build their skills and teach them how to make decisions. This trajectory includes many years of experience being in charge of smaller portions of the company.

The leaders I have met also tend to have had intense experiences in their personal lives, playing on athletic teams, travelling or living in another culture. They drink in life, make the most of every experience, and are unfailingly interested in everything they do. These are people who have made a study of their business from the very beginning, constantly assess decisions made by others, seek advice and insight from anyone who can offer it, and acquire wisdom by seeking learning.

Leaders who are open to input and direction are that much better in their role. As Denzel Washington wrote in his article on the importance of mentors in his life, "Show me a successful individual and I'll show you someone who didn't want for positive influences in his or her life. I don't care who you are or what you do for a living – if you do it well I'm betting there was someone cheering you on and showing you the way."[2]

On Good Friday, 2005, I went to the home of John Roy, former CEO of Roycom (a national real estate pension advisory firm) and Summit REIT. I was there to talk with him about leadership on the recommendation of his daughter, Juliana. I was a little nervous, but was put at ease right away when John greeted me at the front door in sweat pants, a sweat shirt, and slippers. We spoke at length about leadership, but what stands out in my memory is a comment he made at the end of the interview when he talked about his mentor.

He had been speaking for some time before I realized that he was not describing a person he had known when he was younger or starting out in business. He was a talking about a current mentor who regularly gave him guidance. I was surprised at this, given his years of experience, so I asked him about it. He said, "If I want to continue to grow and learn, I must have someone who can offer me their insight. I will have a mentor for the rest of my life."

Lesson #4: Accept and Celebrate Emotion

Throughout this book, I have emphasized the critical importance of putting the needs of your people first, beginning with their emotional lives. If leadership is about getting people to follow you, then accepting and attending to their emotional state is critical. The excellent leaders I have seen are not afraid of feelings – in themselves or in others – but are also able to remain calm in the face of intense emotional situations. They take the emotional impact of decisions into account, especially when a decision may be met with some resistance. These leaders are highly attentive to processes – not just final product – and communicate constantly, because language creates an emotional bridge between people. They also know how emotions influence people's actions, and as a result are able to wade into difficult situations with confidence.

From what I have seen, these skills develop over the course of a career through personal and work experience. People comfortable with intense emotion have had experiences that forced them to cope with it. Great leaders have often spent time working in highly political or controversial areas of the organization – settings where emotions run high. They have intentionally put themselves in the hot seat so they could get used to dealing with the intensity and drama that high emotion brings. As a result, they have the perspective and demeanour required to consider and manage the emotional side of their work. Their own decision making invariably involves good doses of instinct because they are in tune with their own emotional intelligence and the insights that it offers.

Lesson #5: Perpetuate Preparedness

Much of this book emphasizes the capacity to make decisions in the heat of the moment, but forethought and planning are an absolutely essential part of effective leadership. The leaders with whom I have worked have a deep commitment to and appreciation for detailed preparation, and they establish a culture in their organization that encourages people to think ahead. From effective budgeting to contingency planning, these leaders press their people to be ready for whatever might come, developing and celebrating the skills of imagination in themselves and in everyone on their teams. Their ability to be creative and responsive in the moment, which sometimes involves ignoring the plan, never changes their belief that proper preparation is important. Excellent leaders have often had extensive experience with financial budgeting, logistical planning, or strategic foresight in order to become effective predictors of future events. They also believe that being prepared is far better than being caught off guard.

Lesson #6: Be Durable

If nothing else, leadership is an incredibly gruelling undertaking. Leaders are under intense pressure and faced with enormous demands on their time and attention. The best ones learn to cope with these stresses early in their careers and have the habits they need to maintain a dizzying pace without cost to their own well-being. They eat properly and take care of their health, and they engage in some kind of fitness protocol that will keep them resilient and strong. They appreciate the importance of mental, emotional, and physical stability, and they develop these aspects of themselves and their people whenever possible. Leadership is an endurance sport: take care of yourself so you can take care of your people.

Lesson #7: Be a Storyteller

Several times in this book, I have pointed out the importance of narrative. Narrative is a primary mode of communication, an important part of bonding between people, and a major form of interest and entertainment. I have also emphasized how much communication is a central feature of any leader's work. These two priorities combine to form a key quality I have observed in successful leaders: they are good at telling stories. In my opinion, a communication style that does not include narrative to some degree is a mistake. I have seen plenty of leaders who have trained themselves to speak fluently, who have practiced their gestures and posture, and who have honed their use of props and pointers, but who still leave the room dozing because they do not engage with the audience. Every message you communicate is a kind of story, even financial information or the details about how a particular decision was made. Stories are about connecting the dots, illustrating the cause–effect relations between moments or events, and giving the right amount of detail, especially vivid sensory detail. Compelling speakers know how to express ideas and information in the most enduring of forms: the story. Leaders with a deep desire to communicate who present their content partly as a tale are well liked for two reasons: 1) the deep need for information and communication that permeates all workplaces, and 2) the attractiveness of the narrative form. As I said earlier, communication is about emotion. People will feel cared for if you give them information. But how you convey that information matters.

Practicing communication skills is important. From telling stories to families, colleagues, and friends to the kind of skill polishing that happens in courses on communication, improving your writing and speaking is a good idea. This includes acquiring some experience working in front of a camera or using various forms of social media. It also includes being in personal situations where you are the centre of attention, such as emceeing a wedding or acting in a show. Do whatever you can do to build those skills. But in working on your ability to communicate, make sure you focus on storytelling in particular, because that will force you to learn how to engage an audience. An emphasis on storytelling is also a way to develop one of life's most essential skills: the ability to notice small details. Understanding how life works is almost always about paying attention to the elemental features of what is happening around you; effective storytelling requires the same attentiveness. A flair for interesting delivery is helpful, but if you listen closely to someone with a gift for telling tales, you will notice that the story gets its power from the details. Be a student of stories, and when you take a break from your busy schedule to read or watch a bit of the movie on a plane, pay attention to the way the story unfolds. It will teach you a great deal about effective communication.

Lesson #8: Create Meaning and Purpose

Earlier, I wrote at length about how important it is for a leader to give workers a sense of identity and purpose during a crisis. Employees take pride in their work and define themselves based on their role, so leaders should take advantage of every opportunity in times of calm to connect the daily work to the overall goals and purposes of the organization. Explaining how individuals' efforts contribute to the greater cause inspires them and gives them a sense of importance. Your workers are going to connect to you before they connect to the cause, so you need to be the conduit through which they see and internalize the mission, vision, and values. They need you to help them see the worth and meaning of their effort in relation to the purpose and identity of the business.

The best leaders I have seen absolutely love their work and exude an infectious sense of joy and confidence. They live the values of the company. People view their behaviour as a kind of moral compass for how to act. They embody the cause and envelope people in it during every interaction. Coming up through the ranks, great leaders have been passionate about their work from the very beginning. They were the ones who encouraged everyone around them to do their best. They confronted naysayers and spoke out against counterproductive behaviour. They focused on values and set a higher standard from the first day they came into the company. As leaders, they continue to radiate pride and faith in the company's success, and they inspire others with their sense of a higher purpose. Because our work is a defining feature of our identity, we experience a surge of confidence and esteem when our leaders help us to see how we contribute to the greater good in the "daily storm" of our typical work day.

LEADERSHIP SUMMARY

Daily Leadership Lessons

Lesson #1: *Be human*: approach your work in as personal and open a manner as possible, and allow people to know you as a person so that they can relate to you and feel your humanity.

Lesson #2: *Treat people like people*: connect to your employees individually and collectively, and ensure that all decisions are humane and considerate of employee needs.

Lesson #3: *Acquire wisdom and seek direction*: adopt a long-term view of your learning about leadership, and be open to and on the hunt for new ways of seeing issues.

Lesson #4: *Accept and celebrate emotion*: put emotion at the centre of your thinking in terms of decision making, organization and employee needs, and resource allocation.

Lesson #5: *Perpetuate preparedness*: create a culture of foresight, caution, and the capacity to respond quickly to emerging trends, issues, and crises.

Lesson #6: *Be durable*: take care of yourself so that you can handle the stress and strain of leadership and provide a calm, thoughtful, and level presence.

Lesson #7: *Be a storyteller*: develop and practice your ability to tell stories of all kinds to become a more effective communicator.

Lesson #8: *Create meaning and purpose*: help everyone understand how their individual and collective work contributes to the overall goals and purpose of the organization.

Chapter Eleven

Enduring Leadership Lessons

Our sorrows and wounds are healed only when we touch them with compassion.

Buddha

Several weeks after the 9/11 bombings, I had lunch in a Tribeca restaurant with a friend. Like everyone else, we were trying to make sense of it all and understand our experience. It was the kind of conversation happening all across North America and particularly in New York City. As my friend and I sat together, we fell into sharing some of our experiences since the attacks, and she told me a story she had heard that has stayed in my mind as an example of the profound effect of a crisis.

A few days after the towers fell, a young boy and his mother went into a shop, which happened to be near the Tribeca restaurant where we were having lunch. The store was covered in dust and ash, and the owner was attempting to restore a semblance of normalcy. The boy was carrying a small hand broom and a paper bag, and the mother asked if it would be alright for him to collect a bit of the ash and dust. The shopkeeper was agreeable, and then, as the boy and his mother were leaving, asked what the pair were doing. The mother explained, "My husband was in Tower Two when it went down. We cannot find him. Our son wants to collect some ash and dust in case we never do. At least then, he will have something to hold on to."

This story is a superb illustration of one of the basic stresses created by a crisis. In the face of their loss, powerlessness, and grief, the mother and son had taken action. They needed to do something in response to a situation well beyond their control. Maybe the boy came up with the plan. Maybe the mother suggested it when she did not know how to answer the boy's question, "Mommy, why would people do that to Daddy and his friends?" Maybe the idea came up when the boy woke in the night from a nightmare about flames. Maybe the two of them couldn't face another breakfast alone at home, so she suggested an activity to provide some purpose. Maybe it just made sense to find a memento of some kind.

Whatever the motivation, the mother and son are emblems of the kind of shock that can rock people off their centre. Many people had been in direct contact with the New York attacks because the attacks was so visible, leaving them with indelible images of people throwing themselves out of a window or of the second tower collapsing. Many had stepped over body parts as they made their way out of the wreckage, felt their lungs heave as they breathed in ash and dust, or heard the screams and saw the twisting metal and fire. Even now, when the new towers shine brightly over the skyline of Manhattan, those images remain in people's minds.

These were the particular after-effects of 9/11. But despite its magnitude, it is just one of many crises that happen regularly. In my work, I have supported organizational leaders and their employees through earthquakes, hurricanes, suicides, shootings, financial loss, organizational collapse, and a host of other events that put them in crisis. I have also been an interested observer as the wider world has coped with crises of every shape and size. Some people follow sports, and others keep track of celebrities. Because of the nature of my work, I am attuned to disasters and traumas. In newspapers and magazines, on my phone, over Saturday morning coffee, and as I wind down each day, I scan the news for the story behind the story, the one about people and organizations coping as best they can.

Since 9/11, the scope of crises has been staggering. Earthquakes and earthquake-induced tsunamis have occurred in Indonesia, Pakistan, and Japan, all causing thousands of deaths and millions of dollars of damage, along with physical, emotional, and financial harm to millions of people. Numerous tropical storms have made landfall in populated areas. In the United States, Katrina may be the most famous, but others like Rita, Ike, Charley, Wilma, and Ivan have wreaked havoc along the US southern and eastern coasts and in the Caribbean. Add to that the cyclones that have hit countries and islands in the South Pacific and the enormous impact of flooding and drought around the world, and you have massive damage – physical and human – from natural disasters. There have also been infectious disease crises, most notably and recently the Ebola outbreaks in West Africa and the Zika crisis. Add to that the effects of mass shootings, terrorist attacks, and wars around the world on both civilian and military personnel, and you have a list of events with an immense effect on societies, countries, and the global community.

As we come across news reports of various crises in the world, it is easy to find examples of excellent leadership as well as examples of decisions that didn't seem to be about people at all. On the positive side, consider the extensive effort led by the World Health Organization (WHO) to protect health workers in Guinea, Liberia, and Sierra Leone as they coped with the outbreak of Ebola in 2014. Working with ministries of health and other international agencies, the WHO provided educational courses, protective medical supplies, and other occupational health and safety measures to make reduced infection among health workers a priority.[1] Or consider the details of Sony's 2011 earthquake response efforts in Japan. Sony provided extensive supports for its employees and raised or contributed millions of dollars to help the wider community without limiting its own rejuvenation efforts:[2] some or all operations in ten separate plants come back online within two and a half months.[3] We could also look at Mary Barra's approach to a corporate crisis. Two weeks after Barra became the first female CEO of a major automotive manufacturer, General Motors (GM), she discovered that the company had a massive ignition switch problem – one that would, in the end, cause an estimated 124 deaths and 275 serious injuries and require 2.6 million recalls.[4] To address the issues, Barra has been reinventing the corporate culture at GM with actions such as dismissing employees she felt contributed to the mess, clarifying expectations of a more collaborative and open decision-making process, setting up a compensation fund before being legally obligated to, establishing mechanisms for employees to be directly involved in solutions, and meeting directly with victims' families. These are just some of the numerous examples of leaders who focus on the welfare of employees and others in the community while simultaneously strengthening or rebuilding their organization.

At the same time, there have also been several examples of leadership that was less than ideal. For instance, it took three days for the leaders at Asiana Airlines to arrive at the site of a crash in July 2013 in San Francisco. When they did arrive, there was little to no communication in the United States about the needs and status of employees.[5] There was also the well-publicized example of the Costa Concordia cruise liner running aground in January 2012. In that case, the captain's decisions led to the ship colliding with a reef, and his resistance to initiating and leading a proper evacuation procedure led his crew to mutiny and begin removing passengers before ordered to do so.[6] In the end, he was tried and convicted of manslaughter for his role in the deaths that occurred. In these cases, employees (and sometimes not even passengers) were not top of mind when disaster struck.

While any list of traumatic events can be chilling, it also helps us realize that crises happen all the time. You are a person who may end up leading the way through a storm. While you cannot predict exactly what kind of crisis you might face, you must understand the importance of being prepared. The people-focused crisis leadership model illustrated throughout this book is not bound by time, place, or category of event. It doesn't apply only *here* or *there*, depending on exact circumstances. Something might come your way that doesn't look anything like the situations described in this book. And that's fine. Because focusing on rebuilding an organization by helping its people recover their health, confidence, productivity, and sense of purpose is timeless. Every operation in your business is driven by people, no matter how automated or technological some of its parts may be. The basic requirements of the human recovery that drives business recovery are the same for all of us.

Enduring Lessons

In many ways, people-focused crisis leadership fuses the fundamentals of trauma counselling with an organization's need for operational leadership. In the eyes of the law, corporations are legal entities governed by rules in areas such as taxation, ethical conduct, rights, and responsibilities. In our daily lived experience, however, a corporation is a collection of people no different in spirit than a nation, team, club, or group of kids in a backyard treehouse making up a secret handshake, give or take a few million or billion dollars. As a leader of your particular crew, no matter your business sector, product, or service, you are faced with playing a major role in helping your people heal after a critical event. While healing is a complex process, you don't have to be a counsellor or therapist to put the right structures in place. You will definitely be engaged in what could be called a therapeutic activity – returning your employees and your business to a functional state after a crisis – but your expertise need only be in people-focused crisis leadership, which is, at heart, a form of organizational healing. This is why I say that the lessons of this book are enduring: there are basic approaches you need to follow before, during, and after any organizational crisis.

Lesson #1: A Crisis Causes Intense and Lasting Emotion

If you recall, I define a crisis as *a complex and unexpected event that creates instability, damage, threat, or risk to the company and its people.* The effect of a crisis is always measured in human terms. As a crisis leader, keep in mind that this kind of event will cause significant emotion that shapes everything that happens afterwards. These emotions extend across a broad range and include fear, uncertainty, grief, guilt, shock, confusion, and a deep sense of loss. People will be thrown out of their equilibrium and looking for answers. Whatever losses there are, whether the situation was directly connected to people or not, they will feel them deeply and personally. On top of that, your employees will be faced with the reality that things can never be the same again.

Lesson #2: Recovery Takes Time, Happens in Stages, and Is Non-linear

There are many famous models of coping with grief and loss that emphasize stages, but you don't need those specific details. Hold on to the idea that no matter how calm or together someone appears, that person is going through a process that takes time. Different people will achieve different levels of operational effectiveness at different times, while all proceed through a personal coping process. The process will unfold in its own way, and will not fit into a neat and tidy agenda. Even when someone seems to be doing well, there can be unexpected setbacks or regressions. There can also be sudden moments of joy and surges of output, even when there seem to be only sorrow and weariness. Unanticipated moments of insight and confidence will erupt within a general confusion, and then recede. Healing doesn't happen in a straight line. It isn't simple. Having fixed ideas about who should recover their composure, how much, and by when will lead to conflict with your team.

Lesson #3: People Need Control over Their Own Coping

No one expects a patient in counselling to be told what to think or how to feel. There will be support, influence, and suggestions, but not direction and orders. That's because people's internal emotional reality is of their own making, and only they can shape it and respond to what is happening around them. It's the same for your employees. Accept that you are in a supporting role. You can order the number of widgets that come out of the machine, but you can't dictate how people feel. You are on the sidelines of their healing and need to turn the reins of the process over to them. This doesn't mean putting your employees in charge of the organization – far from it. The leadership team is needed now more than ever. It just means giving employees a degree of autonomy and control over anything that connects to their process of returning to work and regaining health.

Lesson #4: Healing Is a Social Process

Togetherness is a defining feature of healing. It is a social process that mostly happens in groups of different sizes and rarely in isolation. This is why support groups are such a staple in our world. Your employees' emotional connections to their families, to each other, and to you as their leader are the foundation of their recovery. These relationships need to be fostered and developed through live, in-person interactions where people can connect to each other: meetings in coffee shops, hotel bars, living rooms, and conference centres – anywhere people can sit and talk. More than anything else, do all you can to be yourself, open and authentic, because every employee's sense of connection to you matters enormously.

Lesson #5: Coping Occurs in Language

Unless we can put our experiences into words, we do not have full access to them. Not everyone processes emotion out loud in the same way, but all of us need some form of interaction in language beyond the typical conversations and stories that happen in daily life in order to do so. Whether focused on the minute details of the event or on the significant emotions in play, people need to talk. The leadership can help by creating times and places for dialogue about a wide range of topics connected to the event and individual experiences of it. Your role in providing people with quality information and communicating frequently on behalf of the organization is critical. The content you offer helps people to connect to each other through shared information and to process emotion through con-versation. From talking with people yourself to ensuring they can talk to each other, make it a priority for words to be spoken, heard, and shared.

Lesson #6: People Need Meaning, Purpose, and Action

Everyone wants to do something in the face of a traumatic event. But when an organization is putting itself back together, only so many casseroles can help. It's up to you to think about ways to involve people in the relief and recovery effort, and to make those options available to the employees. They look to the leadership for meaning and purpose. They need to feel that your organization stands for something beyond its quality products or services. They also need to know how they can connect to its meaning, even through simple activities such as collecting clothing, offering a personal taxi service, bringing coffee to the clean-up team, helping run-down parents with free babysitting – whatever is the right fit for your particular situ-ation. Your employees can become even more committed to your organization after a crisis if real steps are made to connect them to the cause and involve them in the recovery. When your employees come to you with suggestions about how they would like to help, support those efforts as much as possible.

Looking Forward

Children sometimes seem like funny little creatures from another planet, but their basic emotional needs are no different from those of your employees, leadership team, and CEO. This means that they are often a mirror for us about the ageless, timeless, and placeless nature of loss and recovery. In so doing, they can illustrate the factors that have an effect on a person's ability to return to work after a crisis.

In the summer of 2015, a project I had been working on for some time came to fruition. It was the first-ever summer session of a camp I helped to found called FACES (Family and Children of Emergency

Services), which serves children of emergency service workers who were killed in action or took their own lives as a result of job stress. The children came from across the country for a week together in an Ontario camp setting. Almost all of them arrived thinking they were the only ones experiencing their troubles. Initially, they were tentative, reserved, and hesitant to share their experiences or engage in any of the planned events. But as the week progressed, they began to enjoy classic camp activities and build relationships with the other campers. Eventually, amidst meals and races and camp-fires, they started to share their stories and help each other to cope with their enormous loss.

A highlight of the week's activities came when Kris King, senior vice-president of hockey operations for the National Hockey League (NHL) and a member of the advisory board for the camp, arrived with a group of his buddies and a small fleet of bass fishing boats. Kris is one of the nicest guys I have ever met. He is also incredibly community minded – so much so that he was selected in·1996 to receive the NHL's King Clancy Memorial Trophy as a player who shows leadership on and off the ice and makes a significant contribution to his community. But Kris is also a tough guy. In his fourteen years playing in the NHL, he amassed 2,030 penalty minutes. Now, he has one of the highest-pressure jobs in professional sports, which includes overseeing the video replay process for every NHL game from the situation room in Toronto. If a play needs to be reviewed at any game anywhere in North America, Kris is involved in making the call. He's a leader in the centre of a storm every day.

When Kris and his buddies arrived, a buzz went through the camp because of the trailers, shining boats, hulking current and former NHL players, and the thrill of a chance to go fishing. After some initial time spent getting everyone organized, the groups boarded the boats and headed out on the lake. There were two young boys in Kris's boat, one very small and one much larger, but both younger than ten. Once the boat arrived at the first fish-ing hole, the group began getting their rods and lures ready.

As they did, the smaller boy spontaneously turned to the other child and said, "My dad is dead." Without missing a beat, the other boy replied, "I know. Mine is too." Then they got back to work. As they did, Kris King turned away from the group to face the lake because he had started to cry.

Kris told me about the moment on the boat when he got back to camp. It has stayed with me since then because it contains so many of the lessons about healing and humanity that I value. By sharing an experience, those boys were able to safely reach out to each other and ease the loneliness and suffering of their loss. They were able to do it in an informal and low-key way that suited them. It was their version of shared healing. Kris's reaction was equally important. In that moment, he was not the NHL tough guy or the seasoned executive bearing the pressure of the hockey world watching his every move. He was just a guy and a dad. He opened his heart and let the emotion of these boys come in.

None of your employees are children any more, but they haven't changed that much. As you look towards the future, it's important to recognize that while a crisis may come out of the blue, your response to it can be informed by an understanding of basic human needs. Over the last twenty years, all across the crisis response industry, there has been a rising sensitivity to the needs of employees. But there is rarely a recognition that those needs ought to be the *central* focus of the leadership. The leaders I have worked with who excelled at crisis response involved their employees all the way along. Sure, some of them were collaborative and some were more directive, but each was open to suggestions, invited employees to participate in the recovery, and remained connected to their team at all times.

As you finish this book and head off to navigate your own professional storms, I hope the practical and philosophical ideas here can help you achieve a state of excellence. I also hope you will take comfort in the idea that while the needs of a crisis may sometimes be overwhelming, you always have the capacity to do what is required: be human.

In over thirty years of supporting organizations and individuals, I have found that a crisis can become a strangely inspiring event because it illustrates the power of the human spirit. There is nothing quite like what is possible when we come together in the face of loss and devastation. By putting people first and combining forces as honestly and openly as possible, we can heal and grow. We can create a sense of purpose and organizational strength that did not exist before. When the storm comes, exceptional leaders access a deep commitment to community and togetherness that elevates people to new heights and keeps them there long after the calm returns.

LEADERSHIP SUMMARY

Key Concept

• Embracing the central ideas of people-focused crisis leadership means putting the needs of your people at the heart of the recovery process – for their benefit and that of the organization.

Six Enduring Lessons of People-Focused Crisis Leadership

Lesson #1: *A crisis causes intense and lasting emotion*: accept and remember that all your people – irrespective of how they appear – are going through a process of coping with significant emotion.

Lesson #2: *Recovery takes time, happens in stages, and is non-linear*: realize that you cannot direct or manage people's underlying recovery process – their healing and ability to adapt to change will unfold based on their own individual readiness.

Lesson #3: *People need control over their own coping*: empower your people to take care of their own needs so that they can shape their work experience and recovery process as much as possible.

Lesson #4: *Healing is a social process*: create an environment in which your people can easily be together to cope with and respond to their experience since the event.

Lesson #5: *Coping occurs in language*: focus on the need for people to hear, talk, and share stories and perceptions about what is going on and what they are going through.

Lesson #6: *People need meaning, purpose, and action*: taking action to address hardships and challenges helps people to establish a renewed sense of purpose and meaning in the face of feelings of powerlessness.

Notes

Chapter 2

1 Erika Hayes James and Lynn Perry Wooten, "Crisis Leadership and Why It Matters," *The European Financial Review* (December–January 2011): 61.
2 Gene Early, "Basics of Attachment Theory," *Transforming Leadership* (blog), 9 February 2011, accessed 14 December 2015, http://transforming-leaders.blogspot.ca/2011/02/basics-of-attachment-theory.html.
3 Tori DeAngelis, "Understanding Terrorism," *Monitor on Psychology* 40, no. 10 (November 2009): 60.
4 *Apollo 13*, DVD, directed by Ron Howard (1995; Universal City, CA: Universal Studios Home Entertainment, 1998).
5 Marshall Frady, *Martin Luther King, Jr: A Life* (New York: Penguin, 2005), 32.
6 Margaret J. Wheatley, "Servant-Leadership and Community Leadership in the 21st Century" (keynote address, The Robert K. Greenleaf Center for Servant Leadership Annual Conference, June 1999), accessed 14 December 2015, http://www.margaretwheatley.com/articles/servantleader.html.
7 Larry C. Spears, "Character and Servant Leadership: Ten Characteristics of Effective, Caring Leaders," *The Journal of Virtues and Leadership* 1, no. 1 (2010): 27–9.
8 Robert K. Greenleaf, "What Is Servant Leadership?" *Greenleaf Center for Servant Leadership*, accessed 14 December 2015, https://www.greenleaf.org/what-is-servant-leadership/.

9   David Chadwick, *It's How You Play the Game: The 12 Leadership Principles of Dean Smith* (Eugene, OR: Harvest House, 2015), 33.
10   Steven R. Covey, "Principled Communication," *FranklinCovey*, accessed 15 December 2015, http://www.franklincovey.ca/FCCAWeb/aspx/library_articles_com1.htm.

Chapter 3

1   Mary Helen Immordino-Yang, "Emotions, Social Relationships, and the Brain: Implications for the Classroom," *ASCD*, accessed 15 December 2015, http://www.ascd.org/ascd_express/vol3/320_immordino-yang.aspx.

Chapter 4

1   Nicolas Van Praet, "'I Hope I Don't Get Shot At': Chicago Rail Veteran Faces Public Outrage over Silence following Train Disaster," *Financial Post*, 13 July 2008, accessed 15 December 2015, http://business.financialpost.com/news/transportation/montreal-maine-atlantic-railway-edward-burkhardt-quebec-train.
2   Janet Davison, "Railway Head's Lac-Mégantic Visit Panned by PR Experts," *CBC News*, 11 July 2013, accessed 15 December 2015, http://www.cbc.ca/news/canada/railway-head-s-lac-m%C3%A9gantic-visit-panned-by-pr-experts-1.1312430.
3   Covey, "Principled Communication."
4   David Rock, "SCARF: A Brain-Based Model for Collaborating With and Influencing Others," *NeuroLeadership Journal*, no. 1 (2008): 1.
5   Ibid., 4.
6   David DiSalvo, *What Makes Your Brain Happy and Why You Should Do the Opposite* (New York: Prometheus Books, 2011), 16.
7   Ibid., 32.
8   Ibid., 34.
9   Ibid., 213.
10   Deborah Blagg and Susan Young, "What Makes a Good Leader?" *Harvard Business School*, accessed 15 December 2015, http://hbswk.hbs.edu/item/what-makes-a-good-leader.

11 Ibid.

12 Ibid.

13 Dale Carnegie, *How To Win Friends and Influence People* (New York: Gallery Books, 1998).

Chapter 5

1 Tom Spedding, interview by Bill Tibbo, 21 November 2005. All subsequent comments in the book by Tom Spedding are from this interview.

2 Helen Branswell, "Ten Years Later, SARS Still Haunts Survivors and Health-Care Workers," *The Globe and Mail*, 6 March 2013, accessed 15 December 2015, http://www.theglobeandmail.com/life/health-and-fitness/health/ten-years-later-sars-still-haunts-survivors-and-health-care-workers/article9363178/.

3 Bonnie Adamson, interview by Bill Tibbo, 10 December 2005. All subsequent comments in the book by Bonnie Adamson are from this interview.

4 Melanie Patten, "A Decade Later, Hurricane Juan's Destructive Legacy Lingers in Halifax," *CTV News*, 27 September 2013, accessed 15 December 2015, http://www.ctvnews.ca/canada/a-decade-later-hurricane-juan-s-destructive-legacy-lingers-in-halifax-1.1473097.

5 Nancy Tower, interview by Bill Tibbo, 17 April 2006. All subsequent comments in the book by Nancy Tower are from this interview.

6 Lyne Wilson, email messages to and telephone conversations with the author, 16 May 2014, 30 May 2014, 18 August 2014, 6 October 2014, and 24 March, 2015. All subsequent comments in the book by Lyne Wilson are from the author's transcript of these conversations.

Chapter 6

1 Thomas Homer-Dixon, *The Upside of Down: Catastrophe, Creativity and the Renewal of Civilization* (Washington: Island Press, 2006).

2 "Lessons Learned from Transport Airplane Accidents: United Airlines Flight 232, DC-10," *Federal Aviation Administration*, accessed 18 April 2016, http://lessonslearned.faa.gov/ll_main.cfm?TabID=3&LLID=17.

Chapter 7

1 Homer-Dixon, *The Upside of Down*, 116.
2 Thomas Homer-Dixon, *The Ingenuity Gap: Facing the Economic, Environmental, and Other Challenges of an Increasingly Complex and Unpredictable Future* (New York: Vintage, 2002).
3 Jim Harris, *The Learning Paradox: Gaining Success and Security in a World of Change* (Toronto: Macmillan, 1998).

Chapter 10

1 Michael McKinney, "The Art of Leadership," *Leadership Now*, accessed 19 April 2016, http://www.leadershipnow.com/leadingblog/2011/09/the_art_of_leadership.html.
2 Denzel Washington, "The Mentors He'll Never Forget," *Guideposts*, accessed 16 December 2015, https://www.guideposts.org/the-mentors-hell-never-forget?nopaging=1.

Chapter 11

1 "Health Worker Ebola Infections in Guinea, Liberia and Sierra Leone: Preliminary Report," *World Health Organization*, accessed 19 April 2016, http://www.who.int/csr/resources/publications/ebola/health-worker-infections/en/.
2 Brooks Barnes, "A Disaster Spares the Heart of Sony," *The New York Times*, 20 March 2011, accessed 19 April 2016, http://www.nytimes.com/2011/03/21/business/global/21sony.html?_r=0.
3 "Sony Group Support for Recovery Efforts in the Wake of the Great East Japan Earthquake," *Sony*, accessed 19 April 2016, http://www.sony.net/SonyInfo/csr/community/recovery/.
4 Kirsten Korosec, "Ten Times More Deaths Linked to Faulty Switch than GM First Reported," *Fortune*, 24 August 2015, accessed 18 December 2015, http://fortune.com/2015/08/24/feinberg-gm-faulty-ignition-switch/.

5 Susan Carey, Rachel Feintzeig, and Kanga Kong, "Asiana's Response to San Francisco Plane Crash Draws Notice," *The Wall Street Journal*, 9 July 2013, accessed 19 April 2016, http://www.wsj.com/articles/SB1000142 4127887324507404578595730188554270.
6 Nick Squires and Gordon Rayner, "Cruise Disaster: Crew of Costa Concordia 'Mutinied' Against Captain," *The Telegraph*, 17 January 2012, accessed 19 April 2016, http://www.telegraph.co.uk/news/ worldnews/europe/italy/9019688/Cruise-disaster-crew-of-Costa-Concordia-mutinied-against-captain.html.

Index

action: as emotional need, 35–6; and goals, 36
Adamson, Bonnie: on communications, 111, 112; decision to move obstetrics department, 112–13; on financial resources, 97; as leader, 82–3; on leaders' stress/styles, 117–18; on post-crisis management, 135–6, 138; on risk management, 96–8; on SARS crisis response, 80–3, 111–15, 117–18; on SARS epidemic, 79–82; and staff compensation issue, 113–15; on union–management relations, 82
aftershocks, 136–7, 139
airplane crashes: Asiana Airlines, 171; United Airlines, 99–100
air traffic controllers (ATCs), and PTSD, 99–100
Apollo 13 (film), 18
attachment theory, 15–17
authenticity: in communication, 65; leaders and, 65, 157–8

automobile ignition switch problem, 170–1
availability bias, 55

bank robbery, manager's response during, 7
Barra, Mary, 170–1
Bell, Trish, 108
Blagg, Deborah, 67; "What Makes a Good Leader?," 64
Blair, Bill, 158
blaming: emotion and, 24, 25–6, 27; for employee suicide, 24, 25–6; in SARS crisis, 27; self-, 40
bosses. *See* senior managers/ management
Bourque, Justin, 87
brain, 53–5
bullying, 39–41
Burkhardt, Edward, 51
Bush, George W., 78
business continuity: in crisis response planning, 104; impact assessment, 105–6; virtual office

of incidents as, 4; defined,
11, 155, 172; effects of, 90–1,
168–9, 172–3; as human events,
4–6; as inspiring events, 178;
involvement of people in, 4; key
features of, 11; regularity of,
155, 169, 171; repercussions of,
4; scope of, 169–70; and second
order change, 6–7
"Crisis Leadership and Why It
Matters" (James; Wooten), 14–15
crisis management: allocation by
talent vs. job description, 115–
18; and emotional means, 121,
126; everyday, 156; ingenuity
and, 116; openness to learning/
new ways of thinking, 120,
126; people-focused approach
to, 5; priorities in, 76; repeated
traumas in, 122, 126; simple
problems to solve complex
issues in, 118–20, 126; support
for managers/frontline leaders
in, 124–5, 126; techniques,
115–25, 126; temporary teams in,
122–4, 126; TU/M rates and, 116.
See also post-crisis management
crisis reflection. *See* reflection
crisis response planning: audit
of employees' skills, 98–101;
for business not as usual, 103,
104; communication command
centres, 102–3, 104; content
of, 94–5; creation phase, 94–5;

customization vs. protocol in,
92; emotional needs in, 101;
employee involvement in,
91–4, 103–4; employee needs/
support in, 101, 104; employee
skills audit, 104; family needs/
supports in, 101, 104; and
flexibility in application, 92;
goals of, 91; imagining phase, 94;
leadership roles detailed within,
95; leadership skills inventory,
99; media in, 102–3; operational
recovery vs. employee needs in,
90–1; Procter & Gamble and, 92–
3; for return to work (RW), 91;
risk analysis in, 95–8, 104; senior
management trusting local
management decision making
in, 125; teaching/training in,
95, 99–100; techniques for,
94–103; three stages of, 94–5,
104; virtual office plan (VOP),
103; vulnerability/weaknesses
included in, 95–8; wagon wheel
review in, 91–92
crisis response(s): attachment
theory and, 15; community
building in, 20; as complex
processes, 4; connection in, 32–4;
empathy in, 19–20; employee
support in, 5; healing in, 20;
as helping people cope, 4;
immediate vs. long-term effects
of, 76; listening in, 19; and

local management, 124–5; staged
return to productivity (RTP),
134–5
production paralysis, 132–3
professional conduct, 40
progressive re-entry, 127–9
public relations. *See*
communication; media

rail accident at Lac-Mégantic, 50–2
recognition: based on position, 43–
4; increased compensation and,
115; in public relations/media,
44; of specific actions, 43–4
recovery: communication and, 52,
53, 70; emotional contagion and,
30; fear during process, 34–5;
leaders/leadership and, 6–7, 14;
as shared process, 125; stages
of, 173; time for, 173. *See also*
employee recovery; operational
recovery
reflection: and common good, 146;
corporate leaders and importance
of, 142; and failings, 142; and
healing, 141; Procter & Gamble
and, 149–50; and repetitive
patterns, 142; timing of, 141–2;
wagon wheel review, 142–51
repetitive stress, repeated traumas
as, 122
return to production: progressive
re-entry, 127–9; return to
work (RTW) and, 128, 129–31;

three phases of, 127–8. *See also*
operational recovery
return to productivity (RTP):
as competition, 38; focus
on people's needs in, 133;
incremental approach to,
134; as phase of return to
production, 128, 132–5; priorities
establishment in, 134–5;
Procter & Gamble and, 133–5;
production measurement and,
132, 133–4; and production
paralysis, 132–3; staged
approach to, 127; 3Vs of goals in,
133–4; timing/pacing of, 132–3
return to work (RTW): benefits
of proper management of, 131;
children and, 175; and company
reputation, 131; as competition,
38; emotional re-entry and, 101;
and employee replacement,
129–30; lack of planning for, 91;
leaders' own, 130–1; pacing of,
129, 130; as phase of return to
production, 128, 129–31; plan,
129; planning, as if overseeing
high-risk workforce, 130–1; and
re-injury, 129; and short-term
disability, 130; staging/phasing
of, 130, 134–5, 139; in stepwise
fashion, 129–30
Reynolds, Tom, 41
risk analysis/management,
95–8, 104

with needs during, 117–18;
blaming in, 27; and CEO's lack
of visibility, 8; CEO's openness
during, 65–6; and depression,
28; and isolation, 33–4,
68–9; at Markham Stouffville
Hospital, 21, 65–6; and need
for connection, 32–4; at North
York General Hospital, 79–83,
106–7, 111–15; and recognition
of healthcare workers, 44; and
repeated traumas, 122; and
return to work (RTW), 130; risk
management and, 97–8; silos
during, 68–9; speed of onset,
80–1; two waves, 81–2, 138; and
union–management relations,
106–7, 114–15
suicide, employee, 23–6

teams: first-response, 95; non-
homogenous, 115, 116, 117, 126;
temporary, 122–4, 126. *See also*
employee–manager relations;
groups
terrorist organizations, 17
Thomas, David, 64
thought units per minute (TU/M)
rates, 116
timelines, for wagon wheel
review, 146–7
time/timing: fluidity of people
and, 137; for healing, 29; and
progressive re-entry, 128; for

recovery, 173; for return to
productivity (RTP), 132; for
return to work (RTW), 129; of
shared reflection, 141–2; for
support of employees' personal
recoveries, 4
Toronto Transit Commission
(TTC) accident, 42–3
Tower, Nancy, 83–7, 102–3, 107–8,
150–1
Transforming Leadership (Early), 15
transparency, 66
traumas, repeated, 122, 126
Trudeau, Pierre Elliott, 45–6
tsunami, in Japan, 90–1

"Understanding Terrorism"
(DeAngelis), 17
union–management relations, 82,
106–7, 114–15
Upside of Down, The (Homer-
Dixon), 115

values, corporate: leaders and,
166; Procter & Gamble's ethical
commitment, 75, 77–8
Van Praet, Nicolas, 51
virtual office plan (VOP), 103

wagon wheel review:
confidentiality in, 145–6; and
corporate change initiative plan
(CCIP), 144, 148–51; in crisis
response planning, 91–2; crisis